MacRory's Breeks

Also by David Ross

Awa' an' Bile Yer Heid: Scottish Curses and Insults
From Scenes Like These: Scottish Anecdotes and Episodes
The Pocket Book of Scottish Quotations
Scottish Quotations

MacRory's Breeks

And other Highland Humour

David Ross

**Illustrated by
Chris Tyler**

Birlinn

First published in 2002 by
Birlinn Limited
West Newington House
10 Newington Road
Edinburgh
EH9 1QS

www.birlinn.co.uk

ISBN 1 84158 205 0

British Library Cataloguing-in-Publication Data
A catalogue record for this book is available
from the British Library

Typeset by Textype, Cambridge
Printed and bound by Cox & Wyman Ltd, Reading

For Isabel

It's the blue islands are pulling me away;
Their laughter puts the leap upon the lame

Kenneth Macleod, The Road to the Isles

'God gives us this, because we have so little,' said the grey-eyed girl, one time that I remarked upon their ready wit and cheerful spirits.

Amy Murray, Father Allan's Island

CONTENTS

ACKNOWLEDGEMENTS

The contents of this book have been gleaned from a wide variety of sources. I am particularly grateful to everyone who took the trouble to respond to my requests for material, addressed to the *Ross-Shire Journal,* the *Stornoway Gazette,* the *Oban Times,* the *John o' Groat Journal,* the *West Highland Free Press,* and the *Scots Magazine*; and particularly to Joan Gilchrist, Auckland; Bob Golder; Niall Gordon, Muir of Ord; Rody Gorman, Skye; Donald Grant, Aultbea; Anne Guthrie, Old Melrose; Hamish Magnusson; Ronald S. Matheson, formerly of Glenrothes; John Rice, Kent; and Dr R. M. Strang.

If any copyright material has been inadvertently used, I apologise, and will be glad to hear from copyright owners. I will also be glad to receive further suggestions for inclusion, via the publishers.

Ronald Black very kindly provided English versions of almost all the Gaelic texts, and is not responsible for my further tinkering with some of them. I am grateful to Polygon for permission to quote from two poems in Professor Black's anthology of twentieth-century Gaelic verse, *An Tuil.*

D.S.R.

INTRODUCTION: ON HIGHLAND HUMOUR

What makes the Highlanders laugh? The answer is – the same things that make everyone laugh. These can be summed up as Life, with its quirks, oddities, inequalities and oppressions; and Other People, with their endless peculiarities, irritating behaviour, unreasonable assumptions and unfathomable ignorance. But still, the humour of the Highlands – and Islands – is distinctive. There are a number of reasons for this, but perhaps the most important lies in the particular nature and expressiveness of the Gaelic language.

Not many people on the mainland now speak Gaelic, and even fewer use it on an everyday basis. But the cast of mind, and patterns of thought, set up by hundreds of years of Gaelic speech, still show through even with those who have no Gaelic at all.

Another mainspring is the Highland character itself. Now the nature of a people is always hard to pin down in a few words, and any attempt to do so is inevitably crude and generalised. But one might risk saying that the Highland character can be compared to Neapolitan ice cream. It too has three distinct shades united in one block. Its palest tincture, equivalent to vanilla, expresses shyness and modesty. Especially among strangers, the Highlander can be highly reticent. The next shade, equivalent to strawberry, indicates a basic strength – the quietness and decorous shyness do not prevent strong opinions being stubbornly held. Being strongly-held, these opinions sometimes have to be expressed, or defended. The third shade, equivalent to chocolate, is rich and vivid.

Surrounded by friends, or stimulated by the occasion, or with their always-latent pride aroused, the Highlanders emerge as vocal, forcefully-spoken, entertaining and keen to show a love of display and high spirits. It is not just because of the tourist trade that the tartan, the bagpipe and a vigorous form of folk-dance have been preserved here.

Each of these three shades or aspects can produce humour. Indeed it is out of the contradictions they produce in the Highland character that much Highland humour emerges.

This is also why, for every example of 'typical' quiet, straight-faced Highland humour you produce, someone else can show a raucous, ebullient one, and insist that *it* is typical. And so it is – of a certain kind of Highland humour. The Highlanders are not so easily typecast as all that.

In their time, the Highlanders have also been a source of humour for others. The tradition goes back at least to the late fourteenth century, when a rude Lowlander wrote *How the First Hielandman of God Was Made out of Ane Horse Turd*. Such lampoons and jokes, first made out of fear and ignorance, and their modern successors, are not Highland humour, and this book is not concerned with them. Jokes about kilts and bagpipes are not made in the Highlands – except when the kilt is being worn by some quite unsuitable person, or some tradition is breached, as with the knickers of the men of Mam; or when the pipes are played badly. But the Highlanders are quite happy to indulge in mockery – especially in Gaelic – at the more self-satisfied type of visitor to their own region.

A word about Gaelic – many items in this collection originate in that language and I have sought to include items that show the scope of modern Gaelic humour, which is by no means always demure. It can be at least as expressive and rude as the English variety. '*Rann Bhacach*', 'A Back Verse', recalls the once-universal out-house, in this case in the Lewis community of Back:

I was brought up in the tiniest wee
Back-house in Back:

In front of me I'll have a pee
And down below I'll do my cack.

It can also be highly topical, as in *'Naidheachd'* ('News'):

> I picked up the newspaper
> Which I'd have read that evening in peace
>
> If I hadn't lost interest in the matter
> After Page Three.

Much Gaelic humour relies on puns and double meanings, as well as local knowledge and contexts, and its full flavour and resonance can be hard to convey in English. In one or two cases, I have given the text in both languages. Incidentally, the dog story in the first section was considered by its bilingual author to be 'utterly incapable of adequate translation' and my effort is offered with suitable diffidence.

Is Highland humour really different from Scottish humour in general? The short answer is yes, though it would take another book to unravel all the reasons why. Of course, Highland humour shares many characteristics and concerns with that of the South (and even more with the stern and trenchant humour of the Borders). But it is not urban. It reflects a society that retains a sense of space, time and season, a respect for character, and a strong feeling for its own distinctive heritage.

In a not-too-solemn way, this book explores, for the first

time to the best of our knowledge, the authentic strains of
Scottish Highland – and Island – humour, old and new, in
all their variety. Jokes and humorous stories have always
moved with the ease, and often the speed, of the wind, from
one country to another, and their origins can be very hard to
pin down. But in as far as such a guarantee can be given,
those in this book are the real thing. If some did not
originate in the Highlands, they have certainly put down
roots there. There are thirty headings, covering different
themes and including many types of humour. The aim is to
amuse, and to add something to our knowledge of a special
region. To understand a people better, look at what makes
them laugh. But remember also the words of Eriskay's
famous priest, Father Allan Macdonald: 'We're a humorous
people. Better take us while we're in the humour.'

AUTHORITY

In modern times the Highlands have certainly not lacked administration, though up to 1892, most local government was simply the 'gentry' in action to demonstrate and preserve their status (though some may have considered it as part of 'the white man's burden'). When the Crofters' Commission was set up, with its headquarters at Inverness, a joke swiftly went the rounds:

What happens to the brightest civil servants?
They stay at Whitehall.
What happens to the next-brightest civil servants?
They go to the Scottish Office at Edinburgh.
What happens to the rest?
They go to the Crofters' Commission at Inverness.

Other bodies were also impugned:

'What is that floating in the ebb tide?' asked one islander of another. 'It looks like a board of some sort.'
'Is it moving?'
'Yes, quite fast.'
'Then it will be a board of wood. If it was moving slow, it would be the Board of Agriculture.'

In one of his reminiscences on life as an officer of the maligned Department of Agriculture, Colin Macdonald described the occasion when 1,542 Hebridean crofters turned up at the sheriff court in Lochmaddy, which was due to decide whether they were entitled – as mainland farmers were – to keep working dogs without a licence, or whether they would have to pay for dog licences. All were indignant that some stranger should have even raised the question. Their advocate was Alasdair Macdonald, a doughty young lawyer. Since everyone wanted to talk to him before the hearing, which was plainly impossible, he held a public meeting by the roadside. It was one of the shortest such gatherings on record. The lawyer began his remarks: 'A'Chairdean! Mudheighinn Cuir nan con tha'n so . . . ('Friends! Regarding this Court of the dogs that is taking place . . .) when a 'bearded bodach from Barra' interrupted him: 'Mata! B'e sin Cuir nan galla!' (Indeed so! Court of the southerners, as you rightly say!)

The meeting dissolved in merriment. (In due course the Sheriff decided in favour of the crofters.)

*

Gaelic speakers are often entertained by the earnest efforts of official bodies and sociological enquirers to be bilingual:

> Yes.
> We have done some research
> And we have a questionnaire for you
> For you to fill in (if you would be so kind)
> For we are more convinced than ever before
> (In line with our research)
> That we will be able to assist you
> To change your environment
> To make it suitable
> To modern requirements.

May we therefore begin
And study the questions?

Sarglechd ninn
Daltoid niceir fagh ach reighinn!
Spodar ra naosda dàil min!
Caaaaaaarrrrrrr? Sonnnnnn?
Can –
1. Feilean put laraide uainn.
2(a). Miongaiseach rur calaiglean.
2(b). Eichdean.
3. Creis eir liùrach – nodha can!
4. Maile uch 'r aoite dan.
5. Hair dlagh mis pruimpeir (caodan).
6. Utman!

The carefully-enumerated points are laid out in gibberish-Gaelic.

BACK-HANDED COMPLIMENTS AND PUT-DOWNS

The Gaelic language has a remarkable number of synonyms for the English 'vaunt'. Certain things were admired and could be boasted about, like descent from a hero, or skill in music and crafts, or prowess in fighting. But the incautious boaster, or passer of a smart remark, could be very rapidly put down.

A colonel of the Perthshire Volunteers was bemoaning to a local lady the lack of official support given him.

'I have to do everything myself. I am my own captain, lieutenant, my own cornet, and . . .'

'Your own trumpeter?' the lady interposed, sweetly.

A prematurely white-haired man was walking down a glen one autumn day, when he came by two girls, walking along the path towards him. They glanced at him and one murmured to the other, 'Snow has come early to the hill-tops.' The man caught the phrase, and replied, 'And the young cows are down in the glen already.'

*

In the collection of Gaelic verse known as *The Book of the Dean of Lismore,* written for Dean James MacGregor in the sixteenth century, there is an indication that holy gloom was a characteristic of some Scots even before the Reformation. In one of the poems, 'To Alasdair', the poet, Donnchadh Mac an Phearsuin, remarks, 'If grace goes with gloom, great is the grace you have from God.'

*

When Lord Seafield, who had been the pro-Union Chancellor of Scotland in the last Parliament and made the well-known comment about 'ane end of ane auld sang' in 1707, reproached his brother Patrick Ogilvie for being a cattle trader, Patrick replied, 'It's better to sell nowt [cattle] than nations.'

*

Campbell of Combie was an Argyllshire chieftain of the nineteenth century, a man of great physical stature, but, it was said, of correspondingly low moral principles. Not far away lived Miss MacNabb of Bar-a'-Chaisteil, a maiden lady of a certain age and of irreproachable morals. Combie was an occasional guest at her table, and, on one such occasion, he proposed a toast. All the guests were required to fill their glasses to the brim, ready to drain them off in the old style, and Combie rose to his feet. Addressing his hostess, he said, 'I propose the old Scottish toast of "Honest men and bonny lassies",' and with a bow, he resumed his seat.

Miss MacNabb bowed in turn, with her usual amiable smile, and said, taking up her glass, 'Weel, Combie, I am sure we may both drink to that, for it will apply neither to you nor to me.'

*

Another Campbell landowner was standing for election in Perthshire. Visiting one of his tenants, he said, 'I hope I can count on your vote?'

'Oh, yes,' the old man agreed. 'And what about your son, Lachie?'

'Oh, I'm not so sure about Lachie. He was saying maybe he would be voting for the other candidate.'

'What?' exclaimed the laird. 'He must have bad blood in him, surely.'

'Maybe so,' came the answer. 'His mother was a Campbell.'

*

A northern minister was reproaching a parishioner whose church attendances were few and far between. After a time, the browbeaten non-attender muttered that he did not like sitting through long sermons. Nettled at the implied criticism of his pulpit deliveries, the minister said: 'Indeed, but if you don't mend your ways, you may land yourself in a place where you won't be troubled by sermons either long or short.'

'Aye,' replied the parishioner, 'and maybe it won't be for lack of ministers.'

An old Ross-shire man was with some difficulty persuaded to attend a lecture, for which the entrance fee was sixpence. But he was pleasantly surprised by the humour of the talk.

'I've paid half a crown for worse,' he said, as he shook hands with the lecturer at the end of the evening.

*

Two visitors went fishing on Loch Ard, with a local ghillie in attendance. For most of a day they cast their lines in vain, and he patiently rowed them from one part of the loch to another where the fish might be biting better.

'This is too bad,' said one. 'After all the expense of coming up here.'

'I suppose there are fish in this loch?' said the other, looking hard at the ghillie.

'There's plenty o' fush in Loch Arrd,' said the ghillie. 'If ye can fush.'

*

Swift summing-up of a certain lady:
She wouldn't have the infantry and doesn't want the cavalry.
(From Gaelic)

*

An Dìg

If the Ditch is where you live
You'll certainly be in a hole.
(From Gaelic. An Dig, 'The Ditch', a locality in Lewis.)

*

New Wave Concert 1977

I saw a woman
Spike-haired
And coxcombed

Or was it a tale
Of a manly male?
(From Gaelic)

*

Wendy Cope's Cat

There you are, Wendy!
Your cat's died
And you've decided not to make Corrienessan's
Salute out of it!
(From Gaelic)

*

Welcome to the Highlands

Welcome to the region!
When are you leaving?
(From Gaelic)

BAD DEEDS

Iain Gearr, 'Short Ian' MacIain, was an eighteenth-century bandit and pirate whose headquarters were in a cave on the coast of Ardnamurchan. His boat was painted in different colours on each side, so as to confuse anyone who might be looking for him.

The locals liked to tell the story of his mission to retrieve the body of his mother. As a widow, she had married a man from Mull, and had died there. Iain wanted to have her buried in the family plot at Kilchoan, on Ardnamurchan, but he dared not show his face on Mull in daylight. On a dark night, with one or two accomplices, he sailed across, and crept to the turf house where the body lay, awaiting burial. Making a hole in the wall, they bundled it rapidly out, wrapped in a big plaid, carried it to their boat, loaded it in, and rowed away as fast as they could. Tiring eventually, they lay back on their oars, when one of his comrades gave a shout.

'Iain Gearr, your mother's not dead.'

'Is she not?'

'No, she's not.'

Sure enough, something was moving under the plaid.

'Well if she's not, she damned soon will be, whatever,' cried the son, and plunged his dirk into the moving shape beneath the plaid. A terrible scream rang out. Unrolling the plaid, with great trepidation, they found that somehow they had also bundled into it a large otter, which now lay dead alongside the corpse.

*

In the thick of the battle of Prestonpans, in which Prince Charlie's Highland army routed the redcoats under General Cope, a brawny Highlander struggled against a finely-dressed English officer until at last he laid him low. The Highlander promptly began to strip the officer of his gold buttons and other finery, when he saw a fellow-clansman come up to join him at the work. 'No, no, you devil,' he said. 'Get out of that and kill one for yourself.'

*

After the judging had been completed at the Black Isle Show, a farmer whose bull had won the gold medal strolled into the whisky tent. Spotting him, a friend called across the crowd.

'Andrew! Come over here. I'm just buying drinks for the judges.'

That's just what I did yesterday, mused Andrew to himself, as he walked over.

*

Domnhall Mhic Morchaidh (Donald Macleod), who died in
1623, was said to have committed eighteen murders. On his
deathbed he was visited by the minister of Durness,
Alexander Munro, who tried to get him to repent. Donald
was so infuriated by this that he wanted to kill the minister,
but was too weak to do so. He sent his two sons after the
good man, with instructions not to appear before him
without the minister's heart. They followed the minister,
but he had a friend with him, and the friend had a gun. So
instead the two killed a sheep and brought back its heart.

'Ha!' said the old villain, when he saw it. 'I never had a
high opinion of the Munros, but never knew till now they
had the hearts of sheep.'

*

Sheep-stealing, widely practised as it was in the Highlands,
was a dangerous business for the rustler who got caught.
Well into the nineteenth century, the penalty was death.

One day, as a crowd in Inverness was gathered to see the
dreadful business of a public hanging take place, two well-
known sheep stealers watched the last agonies of their friend.

'It's a warning to me,' said one to the other. 'I'm going to
gie up the sheep stealing, before I go the same way as
Alistair, there.'

'Are you, now?' gasped his companion. 'What will you
do, then?'

'I'm just going to buy them, and no' pay for them,' he answered.

*

A Highlander, caught cattle-stealing in the Lowlands, was duly brought to trial. At the prosecution's reference to him as a 'common thief', he objected vociferously, 'Common tief! Common tief! Steal ane cow, twa cow, dat be common tief: lift hundred cow, dat be shentlemen drovers.'

*

Occasionally a bad deed leads to a happy ending, as in the story of Allan Dubh Cameron, 'Black Allan'. These events happened in the late seventeenth century. Allan's chief, Cameron of Lochiel, was friendly with Forbes, laird of Culloden. Culloden was famous for his prudence and common sense, and also for his herd of cattle, a carefully bred strain far superior to the general run of small Highland black cattle. He was bemoaning to Lochiel that he would have to sell some, since his herd had grown too numerous for the area of his pasture land. Sensing an opportunity, Lochiel said, 'I would like to buy your surplus stock myself, but unfortunately the state of my finances won't allow it. But I have a better idea – I have plenty of grazing land. Why don't we come to an arrangement: for a small charge, I will keep the extra animals for you.'

So it was agreed, and Lochiel and his men drove a hundred cattle down to Lochaber. But the Cameron chief, with generations of cattle-raiders' blood in his veins, had no intention of returning those fine beasts. After a few months, he sent his kinsman, Allan Dubh, to Culloden House with a sad story. The Macraes of Kintail had descended on Lochaber and 'lifted' all of Culloden's cattle. Despite giving chase, the Camerons had been unable to retrieve them.

Forbes listened to Allan Dubh's tale, and questioned him closely. It soon became clear that the handsome young man was ill at ease, avoiding the laird's eye, and far from clear about the details of the event. But he said nothing, and invited Allan to enjoy the hospitality of his house. Allan stayed for a few days, and proved a helpful and amusing guest. In the evenings there was music and dancing, and the young Cameron developed a strong interest in Jessie Forbes, Culloden's daughter; something the observant father did not fail to notice. The interest changed to love, and Allan began to regret his part in the injury done to his kindly host. On the day he left, Culloden walked the first few miles of the road with him.

'It's a pity about the loss of my beasts,' said the laird, musingly. 'They were to be the marriage portion for my Jessie, when she finds a husband. I fear now I will have to marry her to old Cuthbert, the bailie in Inverness. No young gentleman will take her without a tocher [dowry].'

The words hung heavy in Allan Dubh's mind.

On his return to Lochaber, he confronted his chief.

'Lochiel,' he said, 'these beasts must be sent back to Culloden.'

'Sent back! Must be!' exclaimed the chief. 'Do you dare say these words to my face?'

But Allan stood firm. He described the kindliness and hospitality of Culloden, and declared he could play no part in deceiving such an honest man.

'I can return them to Culloden in a way that casts no reflections on you,' he said, and at last Lochiel reluctantly gave way.

A few weeks later, Allan Dubh reappeared at Culloden House, driving the cattle before him, all of them in the peak of condition. He explained how Lochiel, jealous for his honour, had invaded the Macrae country, fought a battle, and retrieved the stolen animals. Culloden listened with great gravity to the story, and forbore to ask too many questions this time. Once more Allan was welcomed to the hospitality of Culloden House. Before long, he and Jessie had come to an understanding, and he went to speak to his host. Culloden received him with some surprise, and asked him what his prospects were, and how he would manage to maintain a wife. Allan frankly admitted that though he was Lochiel's cousin, he had but little land and only a few cows. Most of his time had been spent in raids and battles, on his chief's behalf.

'I want more than good birth and a ready sword in my daughter's husband,' said Culloden. 'You are both young. Go back to Lochaber, leave off the fighting, settle down, look after your herd; and if in two years time you can show me a hundred fine cattle, I will add my hundred as Jessie's tocher, and give you my blessing.'

Fortune favoured Allan Dubh, for a wealthy and childless relative died, and he inherited the property. Well before two years were up, he returned, a man of substance, to claim his willing bride; and the wedding that followed was long remembered in the Highlands.

CHARACTERS

In one of his books on travel in the West Highlands, the writer Derek Cooper told of overhearing someone say, 'You don't find the old "characters" around any more.' In fact, Cooper remarked, the speaker was quite obviously himself a 'character'. Such people are much appreciated in the Highlands. If most people are somewhat cautious in their public utterances, the 'characters' are less inhibited. They speak their minds, and, because they are 'characters', they get away with it.

*

In the early nineteenth century, the sheriff of Ross was George Mackenzie of Drynie. His wife, known as Bean Mor Drynie, 'the Great Woman of Drynie', was herself descended from a legal family. Somewhat to her husband's discomfiture, but to the pleasure of other observers, she enjoyed sitting in the courtroom at Dingwall, and was not slow to voice criticism of, or disagreement with, what went on. If the sheriff tried to quiet her, she would call out, in stentorian Gaelic, 'Am I not the sheriff's wife, a sheriff's daughter, and a sheriff's granddaughter?' clinching her remarks by banging on the floor with her gold-headed staff.

*

Neil Gow, the celebrated violinist, was also a notable 'character'. One one occasion he had borrowed money from Mr Murray of Abercairney. As he showed no sign of paying it back, Abercairney resolved to 'put him to the blush'. With a large party assembled, and Gow there at the head of his orchestra, he said, 'Neil, are you not going to pay me that five pounds you owe me?'

Without a flicker of an eyelid, Neil replied, 'Eh! Eh! If ye had held your tongue I would ha'e been the last to speak o't.'

*

D. T. Holmes, who travelled widely in the Highlands and Islands giving lectures on literary topics in the early part of the twentieth century, recorded a number of worthy figures who acted as chairman at his talks. One of them expressed the hope that the speaker would 'feel himself as much at home here as the deil did in the Court of Session'. The doctor at Salen, 'a thin, wiry, twinkling-eyed person', making a speech in praise of James Coats Jr, the Paisley cotton magnate who gave library books to many schools throughout Scotland, said, 'If the donor by any chance should ever sail up Loch Sunart in his yacht, and land among the people of Salen, to whom his books have given such pleasure, I should advise him not to stand too near the edge of the pier, for fear some of the grateful natives might push him over into the loch, in order to have the pleasure of saving his life.'

But not all chairmen were so at ease. Holmes recalled one who was somewhat overwhelmed by the occasion.

Big, bucolic giant as he was, he seemed fearfully perturbed. His hands trembled, his lips were ashy-grey, and his laugh was a nervous grin. 'I am not much used to this sort of thing,' said he, with a poor attempt at mirth and a furtive movement of his hand to his waistcoat pocket, where he had his introductory speech. 'All you have to do is to introduce me,' I hinted, 'you needn't say much.' On the platform he shook so much that the whole structure quivered. He rose, and was received with loud applause. Happily he did not read his speech, but simply pointed to me and said, 'G-g-go on.'

*

A fisherman on Gigha was overheard to make the following prayer before going out on a night that threatened to be stormy:

'O Lord God, my Beloved, if You would be so good as to take care of Jessie and Mary, my daughters, but that She-devil, my wife, the daughter of Peter MacPherson, I am indifferent about her; she will have another husband before I am finished being eaten by the crabs.'

*

The visitor had just climbed the local hill and was dilating on his experience.

'The view was superb,' he said. 'You could see for miles, right out to sea. I think I got a glimpse of the mountains of Harris on the horizon.'

'Oh, I've seen further than Harris from there,' said one of the locals, a bit of a 'character'.

'Further than that? But how?'

'I've seen the Moon from up there.'

*

In his memoir, *A Hundred Years in the Highlands,* Osgood Mackenzie, the founder of the famous gardens at Inverewe, recorded some of the humour of the Highland people. At Gairloch, in Wester Ross, the parish minister had some of the best land in the district as his glebe.

When the minister's corn was ripe, every male and female in the neighbourhood was pressed into his service with sickle in hand, and to cheer up his squad of perhaps not very willing workers he always had a piper to play to them. Before leaving his gang of harvesters to go back to the manse for his dinner, he used to walk forward a good bit in front of his reapers, and plant his walking-stick in the corn, and call out to his squad, 'Now, good folks, I shall expect you to get the reaping done as far as my stick by the time I return from my dinner, so do your best.'

No sooner was the minister out of sight round the corner than someone ran forward, removed the stick, and planted it a good bit behind instead of in front of them. Then the whole gang would start dancing, and would dance furiously until the time drew near for the minister's return. In this way they imposed on the stupid old minister, who on his return would say, 'Well done, my squad. You have not only reached my stick, but gone a good deal beyond it.

Mackenzie also remembered how the same minister had a shieling up on the hillside, where his cows were kept in summer.

On one occasion his reverence thought he would like to pass the night at the shieling, where two young girls were in charge of his cows. The shieling consisted of two very small bothies, one of which contained the wooden dishes with the milk, and the other had just room for the two girls to pass the night in it side by side on a bed of heather with a plaid over them. The girls were in the habit of finding just sufficient room close behind their heads for the big wooden receptacle which held all the week's supply of cream, so that it might ripen sooner from the warmth of their bodies, and turn more quickly into butter in the churn. That night they had to pass in the open; in fact they had to sit up all night with the cows, but they were determined to have their revenge. Peeping into the bothy about four in the morning, when they felt sure the minister would be sound asleep, they noticed that he had hung up his red wig, which, according to fashion of the time, was large, with longish curls, on a peg in the wall just above the receptacle holding the week's cream. So they got a long stick and managed to dislodge the wig from its peg and to drop it into the cream. In the morning the wig could not be found, and the girls suggested it must have been carried off by the fairies, as they were always particularly troublesome about the shieling. But at last the wig was discovered, and the upshot was that the minister never bothered them at the shieling any more.

*

One of the most celebrated, or notorious, characters of the old Highlands was Francis MacNab, twelfth chief of that clan. MacNab kept up considerable style, which would have placed a heavy drain on his purse, if he had paid his bills. On one occasion, a debt collector was sent to obtain payment. The collector was made welcome at the castle, though he did not see the MacNab himself. Arriving late in the evening, he was offered a room for the night, and gladly accepted. In the morning, he looked out and was startled to see the figure of a man hanging from the branch of a great tree that grew close by.

'What is that?' he asked one of the laird's men, who was serving him breakfast.

'Oh, that is a fellow who came here with some talk of the MacNab owing him money. We hanged the impudent creature.'

The debt collector did not wait to finish his meal, but asked for his horse, and fled. When he was gone, they took down the figure, an old suit of clothes stuffed with straw.

Francis had no son and heir by either of his two wives. But it was said that there were numerous scions of the Macnab to be found in the cottage homes around. On one occasion the chief was riding through a country clachan when he came upon two small red-haired boys, fighting. Hearing the sound of horses, the mothers came running out and, seeing the Chief himself, parted the combatants.

'What are you fighting about?' he demanded.

'He said he was the son of the Chief,' said one boy. 'And he's not – I am.'

'No he's not,' said the other, 'I am.'

The MacNab reached down and patted their carroty heads.

'Ye needn't fight over it,' he said. 'Ye both are.'

*

One of the strongest characters ever to set foot in the Hebrides – though no Highlander or Islander – was Lord Leverhulme, millionaire manufacturer of detergents and Sunlight Soap, who wanted to turn Lewis into a modern fishing-farming-factory community. He retired defeated in 1923, never aware that to the islanders he was known as '*Bodach an t-siapuinn*' – 'the wee soap-mannie'.

*

Another chief of some eccentricity was a MacNeil of Barra. It was recorded of him that every evening he sent a trumpeter up to the top of the tower of Kisimul Castle, in Castlebay, Isle of Barra, to proclaim to his island clansfolk, and across the grey waste of waters: 'MacNeil has dined! The rest of the world may dine.'

Father Allan Macdonald, for many years the priest of Eriskay, was a much-loved figure and a distinct 'character' as well as being a serious Gaelic scholar. Of one of his parishioners he observed: 'There's nothing he's so fond of as potatoes.'

'What does he get mostly?'

'Oh, potatoes. But Providence has made them delightful to him.'

*

'Characters' were often people of a somewhat eccentric disposition. Some were slightly 'touched' – gifted or afflicted with a light-headedness which broke down the usual barriers of caste or inhibition. In Skye in the nineteenth century there were quite a number of such 'wise fools', who were usually to be found whenever there was a market or public gathering. The best known was Gilleasbuig MacMathan, known as Gilleasbuig Aotrom, or 'light-headed Archie'. He turned up one day at Sligachan during a cattle fair. It was cold and wet, and the small inn was packed full of the island gentry and cattle dealers from the mainland, while the crofters shivered outside. Nothing loth, Archie pushed his way into the crowded bar-room. He was greeted by MacKinnon of Corrie, who asked him where he had come from.

'From Hell,' said Archie.

'Oh, that's a bad place to come from,' said Corrie, 'and what are they doing there?'

'Just exactly what they are doing here,' said Archie. 'The gentry is after filling the whole place, and there is no room for the poor folk.'

*

Gilleasbuig Aotrom was famous enough to become a legendary figure whose name has become attached to some stories from far back in the tradition. One such story is that of Domnhuill Ruadh (red-haired Donald), and the Skull.

Donald was walking through a wood, when he came across a skull lying in his path. He gave it a kick, and said: 'What sent you here?'

The skull, to his surprise, made reply: 'Speaking sent me here.'

Donald went on his way and came to the great house of the king. He told of his exchange with the talking skull, and by and by the king got to hear of it. He sent for Donald.

'Is it true that a skull spoke to you?' he asked.

'It is true,' said Donald.

The king sent two men with Donald to find the skull and discover whether it could indeed speak. They went back to the wood and there was the skull. But however much Donald asked it 'What sent you here?' not a word did the skull reply.

The king's men took Donald back and reported this.

'You'll get your head taken off for lying,' said the king.

Donald pleaded for his life and at last the king relented slightly.

'I'll let you off if you can answer three questions I will put to you. Be here on Friday without fail, for the test.'

On his disconsolate way home, Donald met Gilleasbuig Aotrom, and told him the whole story.

'I'll help you,' said Gilleasbuig. 'Let us exchange our clothes, and I will put on a red wig, and be you. I have no fear of the king's questions.'

Afraid for his life, Donald agreed. So on Friday it was Gilleasbuig Aotrom who presented himself at the king's door.

'Are you ready for the questions?' asked the king.

'I am ready.'

'How long will I take to go round the world?' asked the king.

'The sun takes twenty-four hours; you won't do it faster,' said Gilleasbuig.

'A fair answer,' said the king. 'Now, how much am I worth?'

'The Lord Jesus was sold for thirty pieces of silver, so you will be worth less than that,' said Gilleasbuig.

'Hmm, very good,' said the king. 'And now, the final question is, What am I thinking?'

And he sat back triumphantly.

'You are thinking I am Red-Haired Donald, but you are wrong: I am Gilleasbuig Aotrom,' was the answer.

The king confessed himself bested, and Donald was let off. As Donald and Gilleasbuig walked home through the wood, they came once again on the skull. Donald gave it a kick again.

'What sent you here,' he said, 'getting me into trouble?'

'Speaking sent me here,' said the skull.

Not all such individuals were as sharp as Gilleasbuig Aotrom. One well-known Wester Ross 'character' fell into the Ullapool River when it was in flood. As he was being swept along he called out: 'Bàthadh, bàthadh! A Dhia gle mise!' (Drowning, drowning! Oh, God help me.)

Then, borne in towards the bank, he was able to clutch at a clump of heather or a bush, and as he held on to it, he called: 'Ah! Faodadh noch ruigeadh tu a leas!' (Oh! Perhaps you needn't bother now!)

*

To Some Tom, Dick or Harry

There you are, my lad!
What a person would say about you –

However much harm and grief
You've brought with you in your time,

It's you no doubt who'd lay claim to the Dick
In any Tom, Dick or Harry.
(From Gaelic)

*

Croit

Dòmhnall Alasdair Dòmhnaill Mhurchaidh –
Nach e bha calma treun:

A' falbh mun cuairts 's chan e dìreach cliabh
Ach croit fhèin air a dhruim, a laochain!

Croft

Donald Murdo's Donald Alasdair –
Wasn't he brave and strong:

Going around with not just a creel
But an actual croft on his back, my hero!
*(*croit *means 'hump' as well as 'croft')*

CHILDREN AND EDUCATION

At a time when Gaelic was more widely spoken in Argyll
than it is now, a distinguished Gaelic-speaking visitor came
to a local school. He spoke to the children in Gaelic, and
told them what a fine and ancient language it was. Then to
try out their knowledge, he asked them to spell one of the
words he had used. They all looked at him in amazement,
and made no reply. Puzzled, he turned to the teacher, who
was looking just as perplexed.

'Och, sir, surely there's no spelling in Gaelic,' he said.

*

Teachers and others in the Highlands, as elsewhere, derive
occasional pleasure from the utterances or writings of their
pupils. Many of these 'howlers' have a fabricated feel: this
one may or may not be genuine. It comes from an essay
written by a Skye schoolboy on the subject of 'Water':

> Water is a liquid, but in winter you can slide on it. In all
> kinds of water, little beasts occur to a greater or to a less
> extent. Even a great amount of heat cannot kill these
> curious little animals. Which is why some people prefer
> spirits.

Another wrote, of the 1715 Jacobite Rising: 'The Rising of

1715 was a failure because the Old Pretender was an unmitigated ass. Fancy an ass trying to take charge of a rebellion?'

*

Asked to define a paradox, one pupil replied: 'A paradox is something which is apparently not what it seems to be.'

*

The Gaelic poet, Rob Donn Mackay, had the gift of verse from a very early age. Born in the days when small boys were still put in frocks, he could not dress himself, and expressed his scorn in four lines, here translated from Gaelic:

No – I'm not to blame, the tailor is:
A blundering fool was he
That buttons placed behind my back
Where I had not eyes to see.

On the island of Luing, a Sunday school teacher was giving a lesson on the Garden of Eden.

'And how did the Creator know that Adam had eaten the apple?' she asked.

'I know,' cried a boy. 'He seen the core lying on the ground.'

*

The fall-guy in encounters with school children is often the school inspector (such stories are the usual way of dealing with feared figures). One of these asked a class, 'What is the shape of the earth?'

'It is round like an orange,' said a bright lad.

'But how can we be sure that it is round?' asked the inspector.

'Did I no' just tell ye that it was?' said the boy.

CLAN SPIRIT

All clansfolk like to contemplate the antiquity of their own clans. This can sometimes lead into the temptation of exaggerating a little.

A MacArthur, a MacIsaac and a MacAdam were debating which clan was the oldest.

'We go back to Arthur's day,' said the MacArthur.

'That's nothing – we go back to Abraham and Isaac,' said the MacIsaac.

'You're just a young clan,' said the MacAdam. 'We go back to Adam himself.'

Their debate was overheard by a Cameron, who interposed:

'You might just like to know I was browsing through our clan history last night. On page 303 of volume 2, it says "Around this time, the World was created."'

*

On another occasion, a Campbell and a Maclean were arguing about the origins of their respective clans.

'The Campbells are mentioned in the Old Testament, you know.'

'Is that so?' said the Maclean. 'Well, the Macleans go back before Noah.'

'How is it that we never saw you in the Ark, then?' asked the Campbell.

The reply was swift:

'Who ever heard of a Maclean that didn't have his own boat?'

*

A saying not found among the Macleans was: 'Like a hound lapping broth are the names of the Macleans: Eachann [Hector], Lachlan; Eachann, Lachlan.'

*

The writer J.J. Bell recalled in his book *Scotland's Rainbow West* an instance of true clan loyalty. One day, a visitor to Macdonnell of Glengarry's castle climbed to the top of a nearby mountain with one of Glengarry's ghillies. As they looked out over a wide prospect, the ghillie said proudly: 'All you can see is Glengarry's, and – and – and all you cannot see is Glengarry's also.'

During the famous visit to the Highlands and Islands made by Dr Samuel Johnson and James Boswell, the doctor was regarded with at least as much curiosity by the locals as he bestowed on them.

'Are you of the Johnstons of Glenroe or of Ardnamurchan?' inquired Maclean of Lochbuie, but lost interest when the visitor was announced to be Johnson, with no 't', and English to boot.

*

The invention of waterproofing by Charles MacIntosh has created occasional misunderstandings, as when a visitor who had lost his raincoat enquired of a group of men in the hotel bar: 'Has anyone seen an old mackintosh here?'

One of the men looked round.

'No,' he said, 'we're all Camerons and Frasers.'

*

At one time, MacDonnell of Glengarry, and MacDonald of Sleat, chief of Clanranald, disputed the overall chieftaincy of Clan Donald. Glengarry claimed to have new evidence that proved his claim. Macdonald wrote to him to say:

My dear Glengarry,
As soon as you can prove yourself to be my chief, I shall be ready to acknowledge you, but in the meantime, I am, Yours,
MacDonald.

*

It was a niece of this MacDonald of Sleat (pronounced to rhyme with 'gate'), who responded to Sir Walter Scott when Scott disputed her uncle's claim: 'Well, Sir Walter, say what you like, but the *slates* are always top of the house.'

*

The Bard of Reay – a careful man

I am a Gordon when in Tiriodh,
When in Assynt, a Macleod be I,
In Cataibh as a Sutherland I go,
When at home I am a Mackay.
(From Gaelic)

COMPLAINTS, CRITICISMS AND GRUMBLES

'Thigging' is a practice that has almost completely died out. Highland pride and hospitality were such that a host could not in honour refuse to present a guest with any item that the guest expressed a desire, or even a special admiration, for. Of course, the guest was supposed to exercise this with great restraint, but some were quite unscrupulous 'thiggers'. One such visit drew forth a powerful poem of complaint from the fifteenth century Islay poet Giolla Colum. He was writing to complain to his chief of the depredations of some visiting clansmen. Their first ploy is to soften up the host:

> Their talk is, 'Sore we repent of our journey here. How true the old, treasured proverb: "The plight of the unwelcome friends who come travelling from afar."'
>
> Then I go forth for shame's sake – it is a regular bondage – and I give them a full handful of my means.
>
> They say to me, laughing lightly for the generous gift: 'When wealth was dealt out, great was the upland you received; no son of Adam has the like.'
>
> Some of them will come cajoling my stud groom, o King of Kings! Saying in whispers: 'Come out here. Tell me quickly a word or two.'
>
> 'Which is the poet's best horse?' is what they say. 'How goes he in the forefront? What is he worth?'

Giolla of course felt it was only right that the great
MacDonald, Lord of the Isles, should pay up for the
misdeeds of his clansmen. The chief's pocket had to be (and
in this case was) a deep one.

On the other hand, the chief, and his sub-chiefs, liked to
make sure that their rents were paid. Along with the rental
payment often went other forms of obligation, like giving
unpaid labour and 'presents' to the tacksman (the sub-
chief). A bitter Gaelic saying goes: 'The tenancy is bad
enough, but the Devil's own business is the sub-tenancy.'

*

The wreck of the steamer *Politician*, off Eriskay,
commemorated in Compton Mackenzie's novel *Whisky
Galore,* was the cause of a complaint from one elderly
islander. Part of his booty was a telephone receiver. The
island had no electricity at the time.

'There, Catriona,' he said to his wife, 'we can speak to
our son John in Glasgow any time we like.'

To demonstrate, he picked it up and held it to his ear for
several minutes. At the end he cast it down in disgust.

'Damn it!' he said, 'I can't hear a *whusper* after all my
trouble in taking it ashore.'

While a high sea-wall was being built on the Isle of Canna, a massive block fell and crushed the leg of one of the builders. Two of his fellow-masons carried him to a boat and took him across to the nearest doctor, at Arisaig on the mainland. When they arrived, they found the doctor was away for a few days, so they set off again, for Tobermory on Mull. By the time they reached there, it was thirty-six hours since the accident. The man's leg had to be amputated. A few weeks later, he was well enough to return, and the same companions who had brought him to Tobermory came back to fetch him. But when they had got him to the pier he said, 'Stop! Where's my leg?'

'Your leg is buried in the kirkyard,' they said.

'Oh, but I must be taking my leg back to Canna.'

'We can't do that now,' said one of his friends. 'It's been buried a fortnight.'

'Well, I'm not moving till I've got my leg,' said the amputee. 'Not one inch. Do you think I'm going to be hopping about on the Last Day, looking for my leg?'

Eventually the limb was recovered from its place of burial. But a new problem arose. The boatmen refused to have the somewhat decomposed limb in their boat. In the end a compromise was reached. A second boat was hired, and towed behind, at an agreed distance of not less than ten yards, with the leg on board. Back in Canna, the leg was duly re-interred to await its owner.

On the Capital of the Highlands

It's a shame over there,
So many Lowlanders in Inverness;
Even if there weren't so many
I wouldn't have missed a few.
(From Gaelic)

*

The Men of Mam

The folk of the Mam wear short breeks
Not caring whether they're black or white;
When they go upon parade
They wear them under their kilts.
(From Gaelic. The Mam is a district near the head of Glen Shira.)

*

A Merry Hymn

The seals have their very own music
Which is heard in the Isle of the Bird;
As each evening and morning
It comes without warning,
It's a pain in your heart (and your backside).
(From Gaelic)

The four lines of 'The Crofter's Prayer' may have an origin outside the Highlands – there is a whiff of anti-Highland mockery about them. But they have been quoted in the Highlands at least since the nineteenth century:

Oh, that the peats would cut themselves,
The fish jump on the shore,
And that I in my bed could lie
And rest for ever more.

FAMILY MATTERS

A croft on the west of Lewis was inhabited by two brothers. They shared all the tasks and their life was such a matter of routine that they scarcely needed to speak to one another; indeed days went by without a word being said. One day, one of the pair put on his jacket and cap, nodded to his brother, and set off down the track towards the Stornoway road.

He was gone for five years, during which time he visited America and Australia, but eventually he returned to the ancestral home, where his brother was still digging in the field. On his arrival, the stay-at-home looked up.

'Where have you been?' he asked.

The brother replied, 'Out.'

*

A crofter was visiting the local post office and store in the days when urgent news still came by telegram. The postmaster handed him a message. 'It's a telegram for you, Jock. Your mother-in-law's dead.'

'Man,' said Jock, 'Don't make me lauch; I've got a cracked lip.'

*

'How's your mother the day?' asked a neighbour of the small boy from the next croft.

'She's no better,' came the answer. 'And there's worse than that – the coo's gone sick this morning.'

*

At the Highland Games in Blair Atholl, Perthshire, a strong-looking but clearly elderly man put his name down for the caber-tossing competition. He gave his age as seventy.

'Don't you think you're a bit old?' said one of the stewards.

'Not a bit, not a bit. My father was going to enter, but he had to go and be best man at my grandfather's wedding.'

'And how old is your grandfather?'

'Oh, he's a hundred and seven.'

'Fancy wanting to get married at that age,' said the steward.

'Och, he didn't want to, at all. He had to,' said the man.

*

A young couple from the Isle of Mull, wanting a quiet wedding, went to Edinburgh to be married in a registry office.

'What is your name?' asked the registrar of the man.

'John MacLean,' was the reply.

'And yours?' he asked the girl.

'Shona MacLean.'

'Any connection?' asked the registrar.

Shona went bright red.

'Only once,' she murmured, after a moment, 'and we was engaged already.'

*

Dr W.J. Watson, a great Gaelic scholar, was recalling the days in his native Easter Ross when Gaelic was still common, but English was taking over fast.

On one occasion the father of a family went to the door at night, and seeing a fine display of stars, called to his little son, 'Geordie, m'eudail [darling], come oot till ye see the ronnags [stars].'

'The goodwife, who was a bit of a purist in language, reproved her husband, 'Don't be learning bad English to the bairn. Could ye no say, Geordie, m'eudail, come oot till ye see the stairs.'

*

Nowadays, whisky and funerals are often still closely connected, but there was once a time when whisky was an essential ingredient at a funeral. When an old lady died on one small Hebridean isle, in the middle of winter, the steamer had not been able to come near for some time, and there was a dearth of whisky on the island. With not enough whisky available to bury his mother with due ceremony, her son became anxious, and scanned the stormy horizon looking for any sign of the *Dunara Castle*. After a week's watching, and no ship, he still refused to sanction the burial. 'She's auld, and it's cauld, and she's thin, and she'll keep,' he said.

Next day the sea was calm, the ship arrived, and the old lady was buried in suitable style.

*

In one district there was a rather fastidious lady of the 'Big House', who followed her social duty in making occasional visits on the old wives of the area round about, many of them widows of former tenants on the estate. She brought some little 'comforts' with her, usually a packet of tea and some sugar. Each of the old ladies would insist on her taking a cup of tea with them, which she was happy to do, except in one case. This was a rather eccentric old lady, who lived in somewhat squalid conditions in a ramshackle little house. She was as welcoming as all the others. But she owned only one cup, which she would swill out casually in cold water before filling it up with tea and offering it to her visitor. The laird's lady drank it somewhat reluctantly, transferring the cup from her right hand to her left, to avoid drinking from the same side as her hostess. On one occasion, she saw the *cailleach* looking at her rather hard, as she sipped her tea.

'I see you're left-handed, like myself,' the old woman observed.

*

At home, there was sometimes no doubt that the wife was the dominant figure. In his memoirs, the nineteenth-century engineer Joseph Mitchell recalled two residents of Tain, Captain and Mrs Forbes. Captain Forbes, an army man, was friendly with Provost Murray of the burgh, and one evening the two sat together consuming toddy. The provost pressed more drink on the captain, but the captain declined, saying he must get home, or Mrs Forbes would be angry.

'Never fear,' said the provost, 'I'll come home with you, and make your apology.'

So they settled down to another hour or so, then sallied out and rang at the captain's doorbell. The door opened, and with great confidence the provost entered, when he immediately received a blow which nearly felled him.

'Oh, Provost! Is this you?' said the lady, who was behind the door. 'I beg your pardon, I thought it was the captain.'

*

Two brothers had lived for a long time as joint tenants of the same farm. Both were bachelors, used to each other's company and little ways. To outside observers, their life seemed perfectly harmonious. One night after supper, as they sat by the fire, the elder brother said: 'James, we're not getting any younger. We've naebody to look after us when we get to be old doddery men.'

'Well, what can we do about that?' said his brother.

'I'll tell you what. You just go and look round a bit till you find a nice, tidy, thrifty quiet widow woman, court her a bit, say nice things to her, ask her to marry you, and bring her back here. You'll be the head o' the household, she'll keep you warm at night, and I'll be just like a lodger, nae trouble to the pair of you. And we'll be well looked after.'

There was silence for a time, then James said: 'Why is it always me that gets the dirty jobs to do round here?'

*

An old crofter was leading his mare home from the moor with a load of peat. As he passed his neighbour Hector's place, Hector remarked: 'It looks as if this will be the last year your old mare will manage the peats for you.'

'Aye, indeed,' the old man replied, 'and if I can't find the money for a new horse, there'll be nothing for it but I'll have to get myself a wife.'

*

An old legend from south Kintyre tells of a slightly whimsical Celtic saint, Coivin, who set up his little church near present-day Campbeltown. Coivin believed in the sanctity of marriage, but not necessarily to the same person in perpetuity.

Each year he organised a special event for couples who had been married in the course of the year and now regretted it. The unhappy couples came to his church at midnight on this day, were blindfolded, and ordered to walk round the church rapidly three times, until they were throroughly intermingled. Then the saint cried out: 'Cabbag!' (Seize!) and each man laid hold of the first woman he could find. Whoever she was, she would be his wife – perhaps for ever, perhaps only until St Coivin's next 'blind date' ceremony.

*

Opposite Invermoriston on Loch Ness was a small property known as Fothar Beag ('little Fothar'), owned at one time by an impecunious laird known as Iain Cinn a' Munaidh ('of the learned head').

Iain was a bachelor and had set his heart on Miss Grant of Glenmoriston. He often crossed the loch in order to court her, usually staying at Invermoriston House for a few days. In order to make the best possible impression, he got a local fellow to act as his servant, and row him across. To hint at an extensive wardrobe, he had his servant carry a bag of straw, at the neck of which his best and only pair of yellow breeches were allowed to show. In the morning, the servant would come to his door and call out loudly, in Gaelic, 'What suit will we put on today, laird of Fothar?'

To which the laird would reply, 'Take one of my pairs of yellow breeches from the bag,' before duly appearing downstairs in his best rig.

If it should turn stormy, the servant was schooled to say, 'What will become tonight of the black-horned and the white-horned cattle, laird of Fothar?'

And he would answer, 'Those that the barn cannot hold,

let the Yew Gorge hold.' In fact he owned no more than a single cow.

At last, however, his wooing was successful and Miss Grant of Glenmoriston became the lady of Fothar. Finding her new abode to be much less commodious than her father's house, she composed a sarcastic Gaelic poem, some of which reads:

O, I went off with the lovely puddings
I went off with the lovely puddings;
I went off with the lovely puddings
And came to the place of lies.

Too bad I am not in a fever,
Never more to rise.
When I arrived at your homestead
Not a stick was in it together.

There was neither house nor barn
In which I could lie down or get up.

*

In his book *A Canny Countryside,* the Caithness writer John Horne paints an often humorous picture of life in the imaginary parish of Knockdry. The dialogue gives little more than a hint of the rich savour of Caithness dialect in 1902. Jessag Shearer and William Anderson are man and wife. The battle for supremacy began on the day after their marriage.

'Which o' us is till wear 'e breeks?' asked Willag playfully. Jessag took it as a challenge, and cleared her decks. It was a tough twist, and the struggle which erased Willag did not take place till years after.

Jessag was ill, and the doctor ordered a glass of wine three times a day. Skilfully measuring Willag's talents, she kept the bottle beside her in bed.

A dismal thirst was on him. He summoned a smile which had long gone out of fashion with him and came to the bedside.

Jessag lay with her face to the wall.

'Will ye gie me a skint [drop], Jessag?'

'Catch me!'

'Ye micht.'

'Ay, but will I?'

'Weel, if ye dinna, I'll gie up 'e ghost.'

'Gie up fifty ghosts, if ye lek; but dinna leave then hereaboot, they're no canny.'

Jessag did not twitch an eyelash.

Willag went out to think.

A fresh line of action was laid: to board the enemy with a rush. He returned to the encounter. Jessag lay still in quiet waters, cool for the contest.

Willag mustered every force at his command. 'Are ye till gie me a skint or no'?' he asked, breathless with resolve.

'Maybe ay and maybe no.'

'Ye'll no gie in?'

'Fa tell't ye?'

'See here, Jess Shearer, are ye till gie me a moothfu'? Yes or no?'

'*No!*'

Not a hair quivered.

'Weel, I'll shot mysel'.'

'Shot awa'.'

'Mind, I mean it!'

'So do I.'

'I'll send mysel' till Kingdom Come if ye dinna gie in.'

'A safe journey till ye; an' dinna miss 'e road.'

Never a wink gave Jessag.

Willag strode furiously to the fireplace and reached down the gun he shot rabbits with. The butt was banged on the hearthstone with a dash of business.

'Will you gie in?' he cried.

'Maybe.'

'If ye dinna, mind I'll damage mysel'.'

'It's a free country.'

No sign of yielding? No; she was but breathing.

Willag rammed home a shot with heat, and stuck a pin in his finger for blood.

'For 'e last time on earth, Jess Shearer, are ye till gie in?'

'Shot yersel' first an' I'll tell ye efter.'

'Weel, I'll gie ye till I coont five. If ye dinna gie in then, I'll blow oot my brains.'

'Goodbye then; and dinna miss yer aim.'

The masterly eye was still occupied with the wall. This stung Willag. Had she but thought his onslaught worth a look; but she declined even that distinction.

'Ye'll repent o' 'is stubbornness fan I'm lyin' in 'e graveyaird, Jessie, lass,' moralised Willag, clicking up the trigger.

'Shot awa', man, an' dinna blubber lek a bairn.'

She smirked. This scourged him to the mad point.

'One, two – Are ye till gie me a moothfu'?'

'Dinna bother me.'

'One, two, three, fower – Will ye gie in?'

'Maybe.'

'*Five!*' And the noble martyr blazed the charge up the chimney. He dropped the gun with a clatter, struck his bleeding finger to his brow, staggered to the back of the door, and slouched to the ground with a shambling thud. A few scientific struggles to the accompaniment of slackening groans, and Willag's warfare was accomplished.

Silence.

Jessag turned slowly and sat up. 'Poor Willie,' she mourned; then giggled. Jerking forth the cork loudly, she said, 'Here's till better luck next time, brave man,' and refreshed herself.

The bottle was once more cozened under the pillow, and Jessag turned her back again.

Willag's teeth fell watery and his eyelids shivered at the suck of the cork, and he was fain to get to his feet, but he remembered that a corpse did not act that way.

The last fizz of fight cooled in Willag's bosom when Jessag spread herself on the pillow and chuckled. He saw nothing for it but to come to life again. A resurrection to reproach was his only choice. Judging it wise to give some warning of his coming-to – more to preface his return than to prepare Jessag – he threw off a few introductory flourishes with his feet, then filled the air with legs. Jessag did not stir, but when he hoisted himself to his feet, she said, 'Oh, yer back, are ye? Would 'e deil no let ye intil Kingdom Come?' Then she sunk her face in the pillow and gave way to merriment . . .

From that day to this Willag Anderson has been as a stool or kettle in Jessag Shearer's house. Jessag keeps her name, and we all speak of Willag as 'Jessag Shearer's man'.

*

Acquiring a wife, for the shy Highlander or Islander, could sometimes be problematic. This story, from the Isle of Berneray, puts the problem in a humorous context.

An old man had for a long time been living with his mother, for he had no wife. A wife was something he badly wanted, but he was poor and old and had nothing to offer. Nevertheless, one day he set off from the house to find a wife. In his hand he took a single grain of barley, wrapped in a handkerchief. He walked a long way, over mountain and moorland, and late in the day he came to a house. He knocked at the door, asked for a night's shelter, and was admitted by the woman of the house. As he entered, he gave her the grain of barley, and said, 'Will you watch over this for me tonight?'

In the morning, as he stood on the doorstep, she handed him back the grain of barley, but dropped it, and a hen ate it up.

'If you've been the death of my seed, it's the living hen for me,' said the old man, and took the hen away with him. All that day he walked, until by evening he reached another house, and asked again for a night's shelter. This time he entrusted the hostess with his hen, and asked her to keep it safe for him. But in the morning, as she was passing the hen to him, it fell; her cow stepped on it, and killed it.

'If you've been the death of my hen, it's the living cow for me,' he said, and drove the cow away with him. When he found a house that evening, he knocked on the door and a girl came to answer. Again he asked for a night's shelter; she let him in, and he asked her to make sure his cow would be safe until the morning. In the morning, though, when the girl let the cow out of the byre, it slipped, and fell, breaking its hip. There was nothing for it but to kill the cow.

'Oh, well,' said the old man, 'if you've been the death of my cow, it's the living girl for me.'

And he took the girl home, and married her.

GALLOWS HUMOUR

The man that was born to be hanged will never be drowned. *(From Gaelic)*

*

Henry Mackenzie, the eighteenth-century novelist and anecdotist, recorded in his private memoirs the story of a North Country laird whose wife – with whom he perhaps did not get on too well – had recently died. At a dinner he gave, his friends were ready to condole, but he said, 'Gentlemen, the best piece of cold meat a man can have in his house is a dead wife.'

The innkeeper at Banchory on Deeside was Sanders Paul, a noted source of mordant humour. When one of his regular cronies was drowned in the river and swept downstream past Banchory before being pulled out at Crathes, Sanders's only recorded comment was, 'That's the first time I've kenned him to go past the inn without comin' in for a glass.'

*

An old Highland crofter lost his wife and his cow on the same day. All his friends came to console him on the death of his wife, and some of them were not slow to drop a hint about possible replacements from among the widows of the parish. The fifth time this happened, his patience broke.

'Ye're aal keen to fix me up wi' a new wife,' he said, 'but no-one is saying anything at aal aboot a coo.'

*

An elderly couple were annoyed not to be invited by the family to the funeral of a distant acquaintance.

'Never mind, John,' said the wife, eyeing her aged husband. 'Maybe we'll be having a funeral of our own before long, and we'll not ask them.'

*

Witches' prophecies should be closely studied, as many have discovered to their cost. One such was Alexander Sutherland, a sixteenth-century scion of the earl of Sutherland. Alexander was ambitious to become the earl himself, and consulted some local witches as to his chances. He was encouraged to hear one of them say, 'Your head shall be the highest that ever was of the Sutherlands.'

Unfortunately for Alexander, this meant that his bid for the earldom would fail, and his head would be impaled on the highest point of Dunrobin Castle.

Norman MacLeod wrote *Thuit Mo Leannan orm don Teine* ('My Love's Fallen in the Fire'):

> *Thuit mo leannan orm don teine,*
> *'S chan eil agam dhith ach luath;*
> *Cha leig mo chridhe dhomh 'n teine bhrodadh*
> *Ged tha 'n rùm a'fàs glé fhuar*

a Gaelic counterpart to Harry Graham's 'Ruthless Rhyme':

> Billy, in one of his nice new sashes
> Fell in the fire, and was burned to ashes.
> Now. although the room grows chilly,
> We haven't the heart to poke poor Billy.

*

A Gaelic Haiku

Hara-cìorraidh:
Tsìorraidh
(Gu sìorraidh).

Hara-kiri:
Cheerio
(Must go).

HIGH JINKS AND HORSEPLAY

Even a little knowledge of Highland history will reveal that in bygone centuries the Highlands were often a rough and violent country. A tradition of duelling, warfare and blood-feud was part of the way of life, along with the more refined aspects of Gaelic society. 'Feast tonight and feud in the morning' goes the old saying. Nowadays, the energetic instincts of Highlanders are mostly absorbed in sport, but once upon a time, things were different. Humour was often a form of insult, and things easily got out of hand.

*

In the sixteenth century, the tutor, or acting chief, of Clan Munro was returning from Edinburgh to Ross with a band of supporters. On the first night, they camped in Strathardle, just into the Highlands. As they slept, some locals, for a joke, cut the tails off all their horses. In the morning there was no-one to be seen. The Munros rode on northwards. But on his return home, the tutor of Munro assembled a much larger force, and went back to Strathardle where, with fire and sword, he made the inhabitants pay dearly for the insult.

*

Not long after that, in 1608, when Patrick Stewart, earl of Orkney, was making himself highly unpopular in the north of Scotland, a party of his men took refuge on the Sutherland coast in a storm. They were obliged to throw themselves on the mercy of the local inhabitants, who were Mackays. But the Mackay welcome was not typical Highland hospitality. They tied up the earl's men, shaved half the head and face of each one, and then sent them back to their master.

*

The long feud between the Macdonalds and the Mackenzies was punctuated by many deeds of violence. But one notorious incident arose out of an attempt to promote peace between the two clan groups. Lady Margaret, daughter of John, fourth Lord of the Isles, was given in marriage to Kenneth Mackenzie, son of the chief of that clan. It was a diplomatic union, not a love match. Margaret was blind in one eye. To celebrate the new peacefulness, her half-brother, Angus Og Macdonald, came to live in Easter Ross, and at Christmas he gave a feast, to which he invited Kenneth among many others. Kenneth duly came, but he left his wife at home, and this was deemed by Angus Og to be an insult to the Macdonalds. An argument swiftly led to a fight, and Kenneth was lucky to escape with his life. In due course, the Lady Margaret was sent back to her father, mounted on a one-eyed horse, attended by a one-eyed servant, and followed by a one-eyed dog.

The eighteenth-century Gaelic poet, Rob Donn Mackay, who lived in the far north-west of Sutherland, relished any kind of untoward event, and immortalised an unfortunate man called Uisdean MacRuairidh, who got drunk at a wedding, had to remove his trousers to answer a call of nature, and then could not find them, but happily danced without them. *'An Brioghais MacRuairidh'* was quoted gleefully all over the North. A small part reads:

The trousers were trampled
Amongst the straw
And Hugh went to dance with
The lassies;
When his drunkenness left him
He took a leap
In search of his trousers
And couldn't find them.
Did you divine or detect . . .
(From Rob Donn Mackay, MacRory's Breeks)

*

A festive night in Badenoch, that didn't go quite according to plan, was commemorated in macaronic Gaelic-English verse around 1899 by Donald Campbell of Kingussie:

Yesterday evening's *feasgar an raoir*
We marched away to Ball Ghlinntruim.
We could not get lasses *cha reachadh iad leinn*
And going without them *bu muladach sinn.*

When we arrived *gun d'fhuair sinn ho-ré*
They all inquired *'Nach tug thu leat té?'*
'We are better without them,' *fhreagair mi fhin,*
But never let on *nach fhaighinn a h-aon.*

It was four o'clock *'s i a'mhaduinn a bh'ann,*
We started for home *anns a' choach aig a' Ghall;*
When we reached *Cinn-Ghiùthsaich cha deach mi ne gleann,*
Regretting the loss *bhith gun chadal's an àm.*

Yesterday evening and yesterday evening
We marched away to the Glentruim Ball.
We could not get lasses, they wouldn't go with us,
And going without them made our spirits fall.

When we arrived we got hooray,
They all inquired, 'Haven't you brought a girl with you?'
'We are better without them,' I myself answered,
But never let on that they'd all said no.

It was four o'clock and it was the morning,
We started for home in the Lowlander's coach;
When we reached Kingussie I didn't go to the glen,
Regretting the loss to have had no sleep then.

*

Oran Mòr

Thathar a' cur deoch ùr bhog a-nochd
Thall an Ionad na Coimhearsnachd.
Oran Mòr *a tha mar ainm air an deoch ùr.*

A-nochd tha mi a' dol
Dhan Ionad-Choimhearsnachd 's tha mi dol a ghabhail
Iomadh Oran Mòr.

Big Song

They are launching a new drink tonight
Over in the Community Centre.
The new drink is called *Big Song*.

Tonight I'm going
To the Community Centre and I'll be joining in
Many a *Big Song*.

*

Cheers!

The lads arrived one day
In the pub
Nattering in Gaelic

And a big posh Englishman arrived amongst them
Full of surprise at their chat

And offered them a dram
And they accepted it with alacrity
And then another
And another and another

And, in parting,
He asked them, perhaps,
To drink his own health
In their own language
And they raised their glasses
And cried out in Gaelic as one:
Good health, you arsehole!
(From Gaelic)

HIGHLAND BULLS

There are far fewer examples of this species than of the Irish kind, and it can be hard to confirm their source as truly Highland. This one, quoted by Dean Ramsay, seems to be genuine. It was sent to him by Mr Begg, the pharmacist in Golspie, Sutherland.

A small boy came along with a message from his mother. 'My mother wants a vomit [emetic powder] from you, sir, and she bade me say if it is not strong enough, she'll send it back.'

*

J.J. Bell picked up another one in the general store of Iona. A visitor had inquired if shoelaces were stocked.

'Shoelaces?' said the lady in charge. 'Oh, we are not keeping shoelaces.'

'That's rather odd, isn't it?' said the visitor.

'Oh, well, they were always being sold out,' explained the shopkeeper.

*

Although the same is told of many other places, there was apparently an inn by the side of Loch Sunart which had the following notice: 'No person will get credit for whisky in this house, but those who pay money down.'

*

In traditional story there is the district known as Sgire mo Chealag ('the stupid parish'), whose inhabitants are as witless as the Wise Men of Gotham. The accounts of this place go back to Iain Lòm Macdonald, the seventeenth-century poet, and probably long before him. In one tale, a newcomer to the village, finding three wives in it who are outsiders like himself, offers a gold ring to the wife who will make her husband believe the most improbable thing. When the first husband comes home, his wife says to him:

'You are sick.'

'Am I?' he says.

'Yes,' says she. 'Take your clothes off and lie down.'

He obeys, and when he is in bed, his wife says to him:

'You are now dead.'

'Am I?' he says.

'You are. Shut your eyes and do not stir hand or foot.'

And he obeys, and lies like a dead man.

The second husband came home and his wife says:

'It is not you.'

'Oh, is it not me?' says he, and turns and goes away again, into the wood.

The third husband came home, and his wife said nothing, and they went to bed together. On the next morning the call goes out to attend the funeral for the dead man. But the wife keeps her husband inside until the funeral is coming past the door, and then she tells him to be rising. He jumps up, naked, and looks about in a hurry for his clothes.

'But you have your clothes on,' said his wife.

'Have I?' he says.

'Of course you have. Hurry now, so that you catch them up.'

And off he rushes, naked as on the day he was born.

When the funeral company saw the naked man rushing towards them, they thought he was mad, and fled away. There was just the naked man, and the dead man in his coffin, and then the second husband, Tomas by name, comes out of the wood, and says:

'Do you know me?'

'Not I,' says the naked man. 'I do not know you.'

'Oh, do you not? I wish I was Tomas, then my wife would know who I was.'

And then he observed that the other man had no clothes on.

'Why are you naked?'

'Naked? But my wife told me I was dressed.'

Then a voice spoke from the coffin.

'It was *my* wife told me I was dead,' it said.

And when the two of them heard the dead man speak, they got out of there as fast as their feet could carry them. By and by their wives came out, and took them home, and it was the wife of the dead man who was awarded the ring.

On another occasion, twelve men from Sgire mo Chealag went out fishing in a boat. When they returned, one of them counted the crew, to divide up the catch, but he could only count eleven, for he forgot to include himself. He appealed to the others to count, and they too could only find eleven. As they stood in panic, the newcomer came strolling down.

'What reward will you give me if I find the lost man?' he asked.

'We will give you any reward you like,' they said.

So he made them all sit down in a row, and took a whippy stick, and struck the first man a sharp blow.

'Mind that you were in the boat,' he said. 'You are number one.'

And he went along the row, saying the same thing, and giving each man a sharp blow, and counting, till he had numbered all twelve of them. Despite the blows they had received, the boatmen were so grateful he had found the lost man that they arranged a feast in his honour.

They had a loch which had been stocked with fish, but when they went to find fish for the feast, there was nothing in the loch but one great eel, which had eaten all the rest. They were so angry with the eel that they carried it down to the sea, and threw it in, to drown it.

*

Iain Lòm's story was that a man came through Sgire mo Chealag with a cow in a cart. The cart was drawn by a horse, with a man walking alongside. Finding out that the cow had been stolen, the people of the Stupid Parish convened a court. After due deliberation, they put the horse to death for stealing the cow.

*

A kindred spirit to these was Wee Jack, who lived on a croft with his mother. It was a traditional black house with only a partition between the living quarters of animals and people. Wee Jack was at work in the byre, milking the dun cow, and his mother was busy making his dinner. She called out, 'Jack, would you like something to eat?'

'Aye, mother,' called Jack. 'What's for the dinner?'

'Would you like cheese, or ham, or tongue?'

'I'm not fancying cheese or ham the day, Mother,' called Wee Jack. 'And as for tongue – yeugh! You won't catch me eating something that's been in an animal's mouth. I'll have an egg, instead!'

HIGHLAND HYPERBOLE . . .

'Is there good fishing to be had in your loch?' the angler asked the hotel keeper. The hotel keeper blinked at him in apparent surprise at the question.

'My dear sir,' he said, 'that loch is three parts fish to one part watter.'

*

In the remote community of Achnashian, three cottages in a line did bed-and-breakfast trade. The sign outside the first said: 'Best Breakfasts in the World.' The sign outside the second said: 'Best Breakfasts in the Country.' The sign outside the third said: 'Best Breakfasts in Achnashian.' The owners of the first two were always puzzled why visitors invariably went first to the third.

At a christening in Pitlochry, the infant's father had begun celebrating before the service, and appeared somewhat unsteady as he held the child at the font. The minister gave him a sharp look and said: 'I hope that you are fit to hold up that child.'

'Fit?' said the father. 'Haud up the bairn? I could fling it richt ower the kirk.'

*

The blacksmith's shop was often a place where men who had nothing better to do would gather. The smith himself was often a storyteller, frequently of tall stories. Many years ago, Andrew Mackintosh told the Gaelic Society of Inverness of one such:

> I remember a blacksmith in my childhood days who was wont in all seriousness to tell gaping rustics of a feat he had accomplished when he was a younger man. On one occasion a carriage and a pair of horses pulled up at his smithy door. The horses had dropped some of their shoes, and a journey of fifteen miles lay before them. The mission of the occupant of the carriage was urgent and brooked no delay. What was the best the smith could do? He chanced to have ready-made shoes, and he requested the driver to proceed on his journey at top speed, and the shoeing would meantime be attended to. Picking up shoes and nails and a hammer, he started to run alongside the horses. Each time a horse raised his hoof a nail was driven home, and after covering a short distance the shoeing was satisfactorily completed.

*

Another smith from Strathspey also astonished his audience. He had a croft by the river bank, and told how he had noticed strange gaps appearing in his patch of ripening corn. But there was never a footprint to be seen. He lay out in the field all night, to watch. There was a splash from the water, then another. As he lay there, salmon after salmon leapt out of the water, snatched an ear of corn, and plunged back into the depths.

So amazed were his hearers that some spent a night by the river bank to watch for this amazing feat, while the smith went chuckling to his bed.

*

Of the Storr Rocks in Skye, the climber Tom Patey observed:

> We had been assured by several climbers that the rock here was no better than porridge, but with a distrust born of long association with rival scalp hunters we had been forced to investigate the place for ourselves. We could now confirm the accuracy of their reports. The rock is like porridge – in consistency though not quality, for porridge is part of our national heritage and a feast fit for a king. This was not.

*

Edmund Burt tells the story of how a laird of Keppoch, chieftain of a branch of the MacDonalds, was out in a winter campaign against a neighbouring laird, with whom he was at war. He gave orders for rolling a snowball to lay under his head in the night. At this his followers murmured, saying: 'Now we despair of victory, since our leader is become so effeminate he can't sleep without a pillow.'

*

'The best cockles in the country iss in Colonsay,' said the captain. 'But the people in Colonsay iss that slow they canna catch them.'
(Neil Munro, Hurricane Jack of the Vital Spark)

*

The compiler of this book, when still at primary school, took part in a competitive discussion between children in a Highland playground. None of them had been more than thirty miles from their home, but they were boasting of how far they had travelled.

'I've been to Edinburgh,' said one.

'That's nothing, I've been to London,' said another.

'I've been to Australia,' said a particularly mendacious boy.

'How long for?' challenged a girl.

'Uh, five weeks,' he hazarded.

'That's nothing,' she said decisively. 'My parents took me on a train tour of Switzerland that lasted for *seventeen weeks.*'

*

A Loch Tay fisherman was talking about how big the waves can get on the loch.

'Surely they can't be all that big,' said a bystander.

'Well, I couldn't say exactly,' said the fisherman, 'but I was out one day and there was one wave came rolling down from the Killin end that lifted my boat so high I could see over the top of Ben Lawers to where a wifie was feeding her hens in a croft in Glen Lyon.'

In a bar in Fort William, a Lochaber man fell into conversation with two visitors, an Australian and an American. They began to discuss the relative heights of their countries' highest mountains.

'Mount Kosciusko is 7,234 feet high,' said the Australian. 'That kind of puts Ben Nevis in its place.'

'Mount McKinley is 20,330 feet high,' said the American. 'I guess we'd consider Ben Nevis a sort of hillock.'

'Maybe so,' said the local, 'but Ben Nevis was a mountain when yours were nothing more than holes in the ground.'

*

An old Highland proverb goes: 'It would be something to one man, but a small thing for two, as Alasdair the Proud said about the world.' (*Alasdair* Uaibhreach ('the Proud') *was the Gaels' name for Alexander the Great.*)

. . . AND UNDERSTATEMENT

During the Napoleonic wars, General David Stewart of Garth served in the expedition to the West Indies of 1796, led by Sir Ralph Abercrombie. Stewart was a short man, and in the course of one landing, under fire from shore batteries, he was alongside the six-foot-four Lord Hopetoun when a cannon ball whizzed over Hopetoun's left shoulder and just above Stewart's own head.

'A miss is as good as a mile,' observed Hopetoun.

'Yes,' said Stewart, 'but it is lucky for me that I am only five foot six inches, or I would be a head shorter.'

*

The little Macbrayne steamer *Plover* was once caught completely unawares in a sudden terrific storm that rose when she was out at night on the short journey between Lochmaddy on North Uist and Lochboisdale on South Uist. For more than nine hours she was tossed about in an easterly hurricane, forced to stay well out in the Minch, away from the island shores. It was feared that she was lost. When at last she made Lochboisdale, a relieved crowd was waiting on the pier to welcome her.

'A wild passage,' said a hotelkeeper to the skipper, Captain Black.

'Och, indeed! Not too good,' said the Captain.

HIGHLAND PROVERBS

Often, Highland proverbs contain a reference to a single place or event, which is then used to describe others. There is usually a humorous intention built in, if only to gently mock an individual or group. The phrase 'Thieving of Lismore folk' is an example. This refers to surreptitious pilfering from stackyards or potato pits. Clearly this was once a problem on Lismore. Sometimes the mockery is more grim, as in the Badenoch proverb 'Meat for your bread, like Cumming's head'. The reference is to a feud between the Cummings of Raitt and a neighbouring clan.

The Cumming chief was besieged in his towerhouse, and when his son was captured and killed, the head was sent to his father, with the words: 'Meat for your bread, like Cumming's head.' In true Highland style, the father replied, 'It is a bitter morsel, but I will gnaw the last bone of it before I surrender.'

Out on Uist, if you tell tall stories, someone may murmur 'Niall na Firin' (Truthful Neil), and you will know you have been rumbled. 'Truthful Neil' was famous for his stories about visiting the land of the fairies. Everyone listened respectfully, but no-one quite believed him.

'We know well every turn in your tail' is a saying used against someone whom you are hiding something from; it was murmured by the inhabitants of Moidart, when they were sheltering Prince Charles Edward Stewart against Captain Ferguson, head of the naval squadron which was searching for him.

Many other Highland proverbs are proverbial phrases rather than complete sayings; they are specific comments for certain situations rather than generalised guides to behaviour. Thus of a miserable old man, cared for by people other than his close kindred, one might say: 'As Ossian was after the Fianna' – referring to the bard's long life after the death of his comrades. Another such was 'Conan's life among the demons', which might be uttered during a particularly stressful time, and referring to the old warrior of the Fianna. When people made the comment, 'The fondness of the Macleods for cats', they meant no fondness at all: a cat was supposed to have killed a Macleod baby. Another phrase to be quietly murmured in the right circumstances was 'Donald Martin's cold'. Donald was reputed to catch a cold every quarter, and it lasted for three months at a time. In similar vein was 'Martin's smile at his porridge' – Martin did not like porridge for three meals a day, which was what he got.

A Gaelic equivalent to a 'chip off the old block' was: 'If not Bran, his brother.' Bran was the faithful hound of Fionn. Other typically humorous proverbial sayings, of more obvious meaning, include:

That's a pair, as the crow said to her feet.

Peat cannot fall from an empty creel.

Whoever burns his backside must sit upon it.

That were trusting a pudding to the black dog.

It is different with the man of the boil and the man that squeezes it.

It's a big beast that there isn't room for outside.

A blind man will find his way to the burial ground.

Though there is a rather sarcastic proverb attributed to St Columba, 'Where a cow is, a woman will be, where a woman is, temptation will be'; generally, women are teased rather than mocked in Highland proverbs, as in these:

You are too merry – you ought to marry (said by one man to another).

Woman's patience – till you count three.

Harsh is the praise that cannot be listened to; dour are the dames that cannot be dallied with.

A man cannot get rich unless his wife allows him.

The hen's wages – her food. (*An ironic comment on the housewife's lot.*)

Numerous Highland proverbs relate to specific clans, and whilst by no means all are humorous, here are a few with a definite humorous tinge:

Ask anything of a Cameron but butter.

MacKillop's invitation: 'Take or leave.'

It is not every day that MacNeil mounts his horse (*MacNeil lived in an island castle in Castlebay, Barra*).

To whom will Matheson be good, if not to himself?

God is stronger than Doideag (*a witch of Mull*). Doideag is stronger than Maclean. (*Maclean of Duart was the most powerful man on Mull.*)

Give me, but let me not give: the Macdonalds' fashion.

*

Poem Number Three

Three things that involve three:
A trio, a triad, and a third.
(From Gaelic)

HIGHLAND RIDDLES

Which is older, the man or the beard?
The beard. (It is older than the man, because the work of Creation was done before man was made, and the beard was already on the goat.)

What is the wood that is neither bent nor straight?
Sawdust.

What is it the Creator never saw, and kings rarely see, and I see every day?
My own likeness (i.e. sinners like myself). There is only one Creator, so he cannot see his like, and kings see one another but rarely, but I see fellow-humans every day.

Four shaking and four running,
Two finding the way,
And one roaring.
A cow coming to be milked – udder, feet, eyes and mouth.

A little clear house, and its two doors shut.
An egg.

I can hold it in my fist, but twelve men with a rope cannot
hold it.
An egg.

Two strings as long as each other, however far they stretch.
A river's banks.

A full bag in the field, with the mouth below, and not a drop
spilled.
A cow's udder.

It came out of flesh, and has no flesh within;
It tells a story without ever a tongue.
A quill pen.

Twelve brothers in a bed, and none at the front, and none at
the wall.
The spokes of a spinning wheel.

It rises higher than the king's house,
It is finer than silk.
Smoke.

It sinks in the heather
It swims in the sea
Fire cannot burn it
What can it be?
A raindrop.

Thin is the skin of your cheek,
Hard is the skin of your two hands,
Your two eyes are in the middle of your chest,
And your flesh is in the middle of your bones.
A crab.

Black seed sown on white ground.
A letter.

A man went to a tree with apples growing on it.
He didn't leave apples on it, and he didn't take apples off it.
There were two apples, and he took one.

With riddling goes a love of teasing. A favourite tease was to offer someone a story, like 'The Tale of the Brown Stirk.'

'Do you want it from the beginning?' the teller would ask. Of course the other would say, 'Yes, please.'

'It's just as well, because the tale has nothing but a beginning, because the brown stirk fell over a rock and left his tail in the herdsman's hand.'

HIGHLAND TOASTS

Health to the sick
Legs to the lame
Breeks to your dock
Meat to your wame.

Health to the one who did not see Calvay.
(*Toast proposed in the Western Isles to the captain of the SS* Politician, *which ran aground in February 1941 on the islet of Calvay in the Sound of Eriskay, with a cargo including 243,600 bottles of whisky. The toast was given before consuming some of the* 'Polly's' *loot.*)

A Perthshire country toast:

> The whisky's gude, the nicht's lang, the weather's weet, and the roads are saft and'll harm nobody who comes to grief. So aff wi' ye – every gless to the boddom!

HOSPITALITY AND MANNERS

The legendary hospitality of the old Highlands is summed up in two proverbial phrases:

> I would give him a night's shelter though he had a man's head under his arm.

> Feast all night, and feud in the morning.

*

Archibald Macdonald of Rhue, in Arisaig, who flourished in the nineteenth century, was the epitome of a genial Highland host. He would awaken his guests in the morning with a bottle and glass in his hand. 'Cha misde thu sin agus b'fheirrde mise dheth,' he would say: 'you will be none the worse of this, and I will be the better'. On one occasion, in the Royal Hotel in Portree, when he was at a dinner and bad blood broke out between visiting Macdonnells of Glengarry and local Macdonalds of Skye, Archibald jumped on to the table and danced a Highland fling among the glasses without touching a single one – the feat restored good feeling among the touchy clansmen.

But sometimes the guest could outstay his welcome. The mother of the laird of Glenmoriston, having entertained a rather tedious visitor for several days, who showed no sign of planning to depart, said to him one morning: 'Be sure and eat a good breakfast now, for it's not here you will be taking your dinner.'

*

The house of Forbes of Culloden was famous in the Highlands for its hospitality, particularly in the matter of wine. The visitor Edmund Burt remarked that: 'Few go away sober at any time; and for the greatest part of his guests, in the conclusion, they cannot go home at all.'

The dining chairs at Culloden House had slots fitted for short poles so that, sedan-chair like, their slumped occupants could be carried out by the servants. On one occasion, an English officer had been acting more drunk than he really was, and when the servants came up proposing to bear him away, he objected, standing up on his feet and telling them there was no need for their assistance, 'whereupon one of them, with sang-froid and a serious air, said, "No matter, sir, we shall have you by and by."'

*

The eighteenth-century novelist Henry Mackenzie knew of at least one house where, at the dinners, a boy was employed to crawl under the table to undo the neckcloths of diners who slumped to the floor, to prevent them from choking to death. Fifty years later, Dean Ramsay recalled the complaint of an elderly retainer of the Laird of Grant, bemoaning modern moderation: 'It's sair cheenged times at Castle Grant when gentlemens can gang to bed on their ain feet.'

*

Highland hospitality sometimes requires the rule of 'family hold back' to be invoked. In the house of Campbell of Ardnave there was an elderly servant, whose name was John. There were family guests in the house, and more guests to dinner. One of the family guests, a young lady, asked John if he could help her to another potato from the dish. John paid no attention to the request. Again she asked, and this time he stooped to her ear, and said, in a voice all too audible round the table: 'There's just the two potatoes left in the dish, and they maun be kept for the strangers.'

*

Professor J.S. Blackie was a great enthusiast for Highland ways and a staunch defender of the traditional ways of the Highlands. Not a native Gaelic speaker, he had taught himself the language. One day he took a friend, the geologist Sir Archibald Geikie, on a trip from his house near Oban to the nearby Isle of Kerrera. On the island, they called on a farmer's wife whom the Professor knew well. He greeted her in Gaelic, and spoke on in that language for some time, but at last, to Geikie's amusement, the lady broke in on him: 'Oh, Professor,' she said, 'if only you would speak English, I would understand what you are saying.'

*

Dr Norman McLeod, an eminent minister and Gaelic scholar of the nineteenth century, was staying in London when he received a message that the duke of Sussex, an elderly uncle of Queen Victoria, would like him to pay a call. McLeod duly did so, to find that the duke was an obsessive collector of the Bible text in different languages, and wanted to hear from him about the Gaelic Bible. To McLeod's discomfiture, the duke produced a Hebrew Bible as the basis for comparison, as the minister's knowledge of that language was rusty in the extreme. Turning to the first verse of

Genesis, the duke said: 'It is a remarkable thing, Dr McLeod, that in Hebrew the article is omitted; it is not, as in the English version, "In the beginning", but simply "In beginning".

Relating the story, Dr McLeod said: 'I just repeated, "It is a remarkable thing, your Grace, but it is just the same in the Gaelic!" I got over every difficulty about the Hebrew by roundly declaring all through that it was just the same in the Gaelic.'

The duke then said he would like to hear Gaelic talked in its purity by two natives of the Highlands. He had a Highland piper in his retinue whom he would call up if the doctor would kindly enter into conversation with him. Dr McLeod said he would be delighted; the piper was summoned and duly appeared.

'This is Dr McLeod,' said the duke.

'Ah, yes, your Grace, all the Highlands knows Dr McLeod.'

Taking the inititative, and addressing the piper in Gaelic, McLeod said: 'Donald, he seems a decent sort of man, this master of yours.'

Replying in the same language, the piper said: 'Oh, yes, Doctor. He's a great man, but a great fool for all that.'

Relating this later to some close friends, the minister was asked: 'But what if the duke had asked you to interpret?'

'I would have given a free translation, not exactly word-perfect,' said the doctor.

*

It is well known that the Gaels do not like giving a disappointing answer to a question. This has proved the undoing of many a walker and traveller who is told that the next village, or pub, is 'just a mile or so' away. However, sometimes the answer is produced by a sense of logic.

'Is this road a dead-end?' asked a motorist of a local, after several miles following a narrow macadam track with grass growing in the middle.

'Well, yes and no,' said the native.

'How do you mean, yes and no?' asked the driver.

'Well, it leads eventually to the cemetery, you see,' explained the local.

*

Em

Hi!
It's just me –
Em I'm just phoning you
Because em because because because
Em I was travelling on the boat
From em Kennacraig to Port Ellen
And I saw em an ad in the cubicle
When I was em in the toilet
To em phone your number
For fun and games!
(From Gaelic)

LANGUAGE MATTERS

This poem, 'Còmhradh', turns on the point that *ann an gaol,* in love, sounds like *ann an Caol,* in Caol.

Conversation

I heard a conversation in the bothy:
Come on, Jim
Were you ever *ann an gaol?*
Caol at Fort William?
No.
But I was twice
In Ullapool.

A Joke

It's become a joke
To her that the current relationship
(As opposed, alas, to how things were

At one time) has gone wrong
Upon us because she said quite freely
In answer to my question: *tha tha tha.*
(Tha tha tha: *'yes yes yes', sounds like 'ha ha ha'*)

*

Lay-By

Under the policy
Of the Council
Concerning road-signs in our area,
The-Loch-of-the-Shieling-of-Making-Love
Is the same
As Lay-By.

Therefore, if anyone
Ever asks you:
What's the Gaelic for lay-by? just say:
The-Loch-of-the-Shieling-of-Making-Love!

*

Biadh

*Biadh à Benni Abess
Is às Abu Ballas –
Cus cus!*

Food

Food from Benni Abess
And from Abu Ballas –
Cus cus!
(Cus: *'too much'*)

Remote parts of the Highlands are served by shopkeepers' vans, calling once a week. The butcher called regularly at Donald's croft, which was up a long, rough track. Then one autumn Donald decided to kill one of his sheep for the freezer. To save the butcher the trouble of coming up, he left a note at the end of his road, saying: 'Butcher: don't come on Tuesday. Killing myself Monday.'

MEDICINE

The old parish minister was much troubled by rheumatics. A widower, he lived all alone and didn't seem, to the ladies of the parish, to take very good care of himself. His parishioners all subscribed to a fund to send him off for a week to a hydropathic hotel, where he could get treatment for his rheumatics, and have a well-earned rest.

To their surprise, he returned before the week was out.

'Didn't you like it?' he was asked.

'I liked it very much,' he said. 'But I didn't need to stay longer. I was cured from the very first bath I took. As soon as I put my feet in it, dear friends, I felt much relieved. And when I immersed myself in it completely, I felt even better. My pains left me entirely. And when I got out of the water – would you believe it? There were the rheumatics, lying like a black sediment at the bottom of the bath!'

*

What's Wrong?

I have no idea
In what way I'm not well
Or what is wrong at all
Just, however, because
I can't read the doctor's
Handwriting.
(From Gaelic)

*

The most celebrated medical family in the Highlands were
the Beatons, who produced several generations of doctors on
Skye and Mull. One of the most notable was Seamus Beaton,
known as *An Ollamh Muileach*, the Mull doctor. A
prominent member of the Maclean family was sick in Aros
Castle, but through snobbery had sent for two practitioners
from Edinburgh to care for him, rather than the local man.
The Edinburgh men seemed unable to effect a cure, however,
and at last Seamus was sent for. Having insisted on seeing the
invalid alone, he saw immediately that an ulcer congesting or
obstructing the lungs was the problem, and that somehow the
patient's lungs would have to be forcibly exerted. But the
Maclean was already in a very weak condition.

The Mull doctor's solution was dramatic. In front of the
amazed invalid, he dropped his breeches and emptied his
bowels into the shovel on the hearth. He then dried and
roasted the contents of the shovel on the fire, until they could
be reduced easily to a powder. The powder was wrapped in
paper and placed, part-open, on the bedside table. Not a
word was spoken in all this. Then, without any instructions
to Maclean, the doctor left, merely saying he would return
next day. As soon as he was gone, the other two doctors
hurried officiously in, to find out what had been happening.
The patient pointed to the packet of brownish powder, and
explained that Beaton had left it, without any instructions.
Seizing it, they examined it, poked their fingers into it,
sniffed at it, licked their fingers, sampled it like snuff, even
ate some of it. The sight of all this was too much for the
patient. He broke into laughter, so heartily that the ulcer
burst, and he coughed up the congestant stuff. Shortly after
that, Seamus Beaton was able to complete the cure.

*

The pride taken by the Highlanders in their medical
tradition is shown by another Beaton tale. In this case it was

a king who was taken ill. Once again, the city doctors were unable to provide a diagnosis, let alone a cure. On the advice of one of his counsellors, the king sent for one of the Beatons. This man had a great reputation for making inferences from urine samples. But when the northern doctor arrived, his urban colleagues, jealous of their positions and anxious to show up the country bumpkin, substituted a phial of cow's urine for that of the king. Holding the vessel to the light, as they waited for his word, the ollamh scrutinised it for a long time, and did not forbear to sniff, and even insert the finger. Eventually he turned to the other doctors and said:

'If you gentlemen will open up his majesty, you will find him in calf.'

MIDGES

An enigmatic Highland proverb says: 'The cow is only a good deal bigger than the midge.' Midges are one of the things Highlanders are sensitive about, as well as sensitive to. They know that the little beasties are unpopular with visitors. Tourists who accept the weather without complaint can be driven into frenzy by the midges. Highlanders, being too kind to rub salt into the wounds, tend to keep midge jokes to themselves.

They tell of a German cyclist who cried out in exasperation: 'Unheimlich! Each time I kill one, ten thousand come to its funeral.'

And of a troop of English boy scouts who found their camp site was deep into midge country. As the evening darkened, an itching Tenderfoot saw fireflies begin to appear.

'Oh no,' he cried in despair, 'they've got searchlight support.'

*

The last word on midges was had by Neil Munro, the Argyllshire writer who as 'Hugh Foulis' wrote the famous 'Para Handy' stories about the misadventures of the crew of a West Coast puffer, the *Vital Spark*:

> 'The Congo's not to be compared wi' the West o' Scotland when it comes to insects,' said Para Handy. 'There's places here that's chust deplorable whenever the weather's the least bit warm. Look at Tighnabruaich! – they're that bad there, they'll bite their way through corrugated iron roofs to get at ye! Take Clynder, again, or any other place in the Gareloch, and ye'll see the old ones leadin' roond the young ones, learnin' them the proper grips. There iss a spashial kind of mudge in Dervaig, in the Isle of Mull, that hass aal the points of a Poltalloch terrier, even to the black nose and the cocked lugs, and sits up and barks at you.'

He went on to mention the midges of Colonsay, so big you could throw stones at them. But Para Handy's suggested anti-midge protection, golden syrup spread over the face, is not perhaps to be recommended.

MINISTERS AND RELIGION

Even nowadays, ministers of the church have rather more standing in the Highlands than in other parts of the country. This does not debar them from criticism, however, including from their brethren of the cloth.

*

There was one family which boasted three ministers in succession, grandfather, father and son. The general view was that with each successive generation, the original ability had become watered down. When someone remarked to a fellow minister that he had heard the grandson preaching a sermon, the minister asked: 'What kind of a sermon was it? If it had both manner and matter it would be from his grandfather. If it had manner but no matter, it would be his father's; and if it had neither manner nor matter, it would be all his own work.'

Several proverbs exist to remind ministers of their human weakness:

God has not said all you have said.

It is not the priest's first story that should be believed.

The justice of the clergy to each other.

Hard as is the factor's rule, no better is the minister's.

*

The one-time minister at Foyers, on the east side of Loch Ness, the Rev. Mr Howieson, fell out with some of his parishioners, whom he had had to rebuke for unruly behaviour. One Sunday, after the church service, several of them waited for him on the way home. They asked for his help, since one of them owned a pony that was about to be taken from him to pay a debt. If the minister would only take it into his ownership, for a nominal sum, say sixpence, the creditor would not get it. The minister agreed and paid the sixpence to buy the pony. But it was a trap. He found himself reported to the presbytery for profaning the Sabbath by doing business. After that, it is said, his mouth was closed for a time.

*

A new minister was called, as the phrase goes, meaning chosen by the kirk session, to a West Highland parish. His sermons and conduct of the service were exemplary. But it became known that he was in the habit of taking a walk on Sunday afternoon. One of the kirk elders confronted him on a Monday morning.

'Is it true, Minister, that you take walks on the Sabbath Day?'

'Indeed it is,' said the minister.

'But the commandment says, 'Remember the Sabbath Day, and keep it holy.''

Gently the minister mentioned that Christ Himself is recorded as having gone out walking on Sunday. The elder was defeated, but not struck dumb.

'I never thought the better of Him for it, though,' he said.

*

On Tiree there was a wandering, gipsyish fellow whom was never seen in the island church. One day the minister accosted him and asked him why he did not come.

'It's that I have no good trousers to wear,' said the man.

'Come to the church and you'll get trousers,' said the minister.

The man duly came on the following Sunday. After the service, the minister took him aside, and engaged in lengthy prayers for the man's soul. After a while he paused, and said to the man, hoping he might have felt some spiritual benefit:

'Did you get anything?'

'I thought it was yourself who would be giving me the trousers,' said the man, in surprise.

*

Some ministers had a reassuring humility, like the Rev. Kenneth McLeod, of Gigha, author of *The Road to the Isles* and translator of many Gaelic songs.

'Only the good die young, so we're all right', was a favourite saying of his. On one occasion, à propos of an ostentatiously holy young man, he murmured: 'I'm always suspicious of a man who never drinks or smokes or goes with a girl – and who likes cocoa!'

*

Cùram

I've not got the *Cùram*, not a bit of it,
Thanks be to the Lord.
(From Gaelic. Cùram: *literally the state of spiritual 'concern' that follows religious conversion.)*

*

Thought

Nietszche is on the Way of Truth,
Said God (lately departed).
(From Gaelic)

MISCELLANEOUS OBSERVATIONS

Perhaps the earliest recorded humorous events in the Highlands are told in *The Life of St Columba,* written by a fellow-saint, and abbot of Iona, Adamnan, around AD 700. On one occasion, sitting with the monks of Iona, Columba began to smile. When asked why, he said: 'Columban, son of Beogna, just starting to sail over to us, is now in great danger in the rolling tides of the Corrievreckan Whirlpool. Sitting in the prow, he holds both hands up to heaven and yet blesses the stormy and threatening sea. The Lord is putting fear on him, not because he is to be overwhelmed in the waves, but rather that he may be roused to pray even more earnestly that the Lord will give him a safe passage to us.'

The saint was sitting writing in his cell, with his attendant Diormit by him, when there came a loud 'Halloo!' as someone called from the mainland for a boat. The saint said: 'The man who is shouting beyond the strait is not a man of refined sentiment, for today he will upset and spill my ink-horn.'

Diormit resolved to keep a close watch to guard the ink-horn. But he had to leave the cell for some purpose or other, and while he was away the stranger arrived, and in eager haste to kiss the holy abbot, upset the ink-horn, overturned by the skirt of his garment.

*

The Food Chain

Seven herrings the salmon's meal,
Seven salmon the feast of seal,
Seven seals for the small sow-whale,
Seven small whales the big regale,
Seven big whales to Kraken given,
Leviathan takes Kraken seven.
(From Gaelic)

A lady who used to visit Colonsay each year for the Young Farmer's Club annual Root, Grain and Produce Show at Kiloran, was looking on at the judging of the live hens. This was carried out by a lady judge, Poultry Adviser to the West of Scotland Agricultural College. Suddenly, a hen got away from the judge and took to its heels, fluttering off with the judge in hot pursuit. The judge was faster, but the hen was better at dodging. As they raced around, one of the bystanders remarked: 'I don't know why she's bothering – it can't get off the island.'

*

A comic poem by the Lewis writer Norman MacLeod, '*An "Sus" a Shàraich Mi*' ('The "Sus" That Vexed Me'), relates what happened when his lady-friend's suspender belt broke while they were strolling together. He places his foot on the trailing hook while she tries to pull away. All that happens is that he falls flat:

> 'That's enough of that,' I said to her
> As I sat up, much annoyed:
> I closed my eyes and made a grab
> At the 'sus' above her knees.
> That wick contained elastic
> And it jumped out of my hand
> And gave a skelp to something
> That's much treasured by a virgin.

*

A family living on the Shetland isle of Bressay, in the days when toilets were in a 'wee hoose' out the back, had theirs in a shed reached by a few wooden steps. They referred to this outhouse, politely, as 'The Necessary'. Once they had a problem when their shed was infested by rats, and wrote to the Council for advice. To their consternation, a letter came back from a Council official promising that he would come 'and take the necessary steps'.

*

A Perthshire farmer was ploughing a field which bordered on a narrow road, when a country lad came up and accosted him.

'I've coupit my cart, man,' said the lad.

'Coupit yer cart? Man, that's a pity. What had ye on't?'

'A big load o' hay. Do you think you could maybe come and help me lift it?'

'Weel, I canna just leave my horses in the middle o' the field, but as soon's I get doon to the end o' the furra, I'll come and ha'e a look.'

'Man, d'ye no think ye could come i' the noo?'

'I' the noo? Ye see weel eneuch that I canna.'

'Aweel,' said the lad, 'if ye canna come i' the noo, there's naething for't; I'll ha'e til wait. But the hanged thing is, my faither's underneath it.'

There is only one large town in the Highlands, and that is the city of Inverness. As a metropolis, with all the allurements of urban life, it is often regarded with some dubiety by the country dwellers. One young man, about to join a mission visit to Indonesia, was going the rounds of his native parish, saying goodbye. An elderly resident grasped his hands, gazed into his eyes, and said warmly: 'I don't like at all to think of you going amongst such people as these.'

'What have you got against the Indonesians?' asked the missionary.

'Oh, is it the Indonesians? I thought I heard you were going to be among the *Invernesians*.'

MUSIC

At times of leisure, the Highlanders are likely to be at their most uninhibited.

The writer and naturalist Seton Gordon was once told of a village concert somewhere on the Isle of Skye. The chairman of the event rose to introduce the next performer, a piper. As he sat down again, and the musician was adjusting his instrument, a voice from the back row called: 'He's just a damned fool.'

The chairman sprang to his feet.

'Who called the piper a damned fool?' he demanded.

Back came the retort:

'Who called the damned fool a piper?'

*

Pipers of distinction have always been greatly esteemed. At an anglers' inn in the West Highlands, an eminent company had assembled for a week's fishing. It comprised two cabinet ministers, a bishop, and a High Court judge. At the end of an excellent dinner, the bishop leant back in his chair, and, with some unction, said to the landlord: 'Well, Alastair, I expect it's a long time since you had such a distinguished quartet staying in your hotel.'

'Not at all, not at all,' replied the landlord. 'Why, only the week before last we had four pipers staying here, and every one of them a gold medallist at the Northern Meeting.'

*

The tenant of a castle, having rented it for the shooting season, also had the benefit of the services of the laird's piper, Lachlan. At the end of dinner, the piper would come in and play a pibroch. The butler always had a large glass of whisky standing ready, which Lachlan would down quickly. But on the third evening, the tenant forbade the glass, unwilling to see his expensive malt whisky given to a mere piper. The playing that night was execrable. Even the tenant could tell that something was amiss.

'What is the matter with your piping tonight, Lachlan?' asked one of the guests, who knew him.

'Oh, the pipes are hard tonight,' said Lachlan, his eye on the tenant. 'Terrible hard. They need softening.'

'How do you soften them?' asked the tenant.

'They need malt whisky,' replied Lachlan.

Somewhat reluctantly, the tenant ordered a glass of malt whisky to be brought, and Lachlan swiftly downed it.

'But I thought you said it was for the pipes!' expostulated the tenant.

'Indeed and it is,' said Lachlan. 'But the thing is, you have to blaw it into them.'

*

'Sticky-fingered' is an insult pipers from the North will sometimes throw at a bagpipe player from south of the Highland Line. It comes from an occasion when Iain Dall Mackay, 'Blind Ian', was a pupil at the MacCrimmon piping college on Skye. After supper one day, Iain had played a piece, and had been followed by a piper from the South. The master asked the second player why he had not played like Iain Dall. 'By St Mary,' the lad said, 'I'd do so if my fingers had not been after the skate,' alluding to the fish they had had for supper.

*

One of the MacCrimmons, Padruig Caogach, 'Squinting Patrick', composed a tune which he never finished. It was known as '*Am Port Leathach*', 'The Half-Tune', and was very popular despite its incomplete state. Iain Dall finished it, and called the result '*Lasan Phadruig Chaogach*', 'The Wrath of Squinting Patrick', anticipating the reaction of the composer. Indeed, the indignant Patrick pushed the presumptuous Iain over a cliff, but luckily he fell on a ledge a little way down, and was rescued unhurt.

*

Another of the MacCrimmons had a special way of making sure his pupils memorised their tunes. He would take them down to the beach. There, at low tide, he would mark the notes in the sand. If they had not perfected the tune by the time the incoming tide had covered the notes, he sent them home.

*

Another of the same clan wrote a song whose chorus was:

Oh, for three hands –
One for the claymore, and two for the pipes!

Here is where the Highlanders get their own back on all the terrible anti-bagpipe jokes.

Sanders MacGillivray had gone to visit London for the first time, and when he came back, all his friends in the glen were keen to find out how he had liked the great city.

'Did you like it, Sanders?'

'Aye, it was not bad,' said Sanders.

'As good as that, eh?' said someone wistfully.

'And how did you get on, down there among the English?'

'Not too bad,' said Sanders. 'But they're strange people. They don't go to bed at night. There I was in the hotel room, at two o' clock in the morning, and there was a whole crowd outside my door, shouting and banging away.'

'What did you do, Sanders?' everyone asked.

'I just kept on playing my bagpipes.'

*

Although the bagpipe and the violin were both favourite instruments in the Highlands, the arrival of the pianoforte was regarded with some suspicion by men of the old school. It was regarded as suitable for girls. But when boys and young men also began to learn to play it, some of their elders were affronted.

'Can the cratur do sewing, as weel?' inquired one such, visiting a relative's home and seeing the son of the house seated at the keyboard.

SAVING SAYINGS

If the butter has no hairs in it, then the cow will not thrive.

A clean kitchen is a token of poor housekeeping.

Leave a clean house behind you, and the new tenant will have bad luck.

The mair dirt, the less hurt.

Sweep the yard, and the cows will just manure it again.

The clartier, the cosier.

Rain through the roof washes out the soot.

TOURISTS

One day an inhabitant of Eriskay, who acted as a sort of general handyman to the island's priest, saw some visitors on the beach, bathing from the silver sands. When they came out of the water, they began to bend down and touch their toes, in what appeared to be a ritual gesture.

'Sun-worshipping pagans,' said the man to himself, in horror, and ran to tell the priest, who gently informed him about physical exercises.

*

In the 1920s, when St Kilda was still inhabited, the islanders were accustomed to having visitors come out on the ship that called monthly with supplies, the *Hebrides*. Usually these visitors were English, ignorant of Gaelic, and the impoverished islanders regarded them as fair game. On one occasion, among the visitors was a Ross-shire man, Colin Macdonald (who told the story), and the new district nurse, who was a remarkably plain woman. As they were being rowed from the ship to the Village landing, by an old man and a youth, the youth eyed up the passengers and said to the old man, in Gaelic: 'Ciod e chuiridh sinn orra, saoil sibh?' (What will we charge them, do you think?)

'Fiachaidh sinn da thasdan,' We'll try two shillings, was

the answer, and the old man promptly put his hat in front of the nurse and said: 'Two shillings, mem.'

'Two shillings!' exclaimed the nurse. 'Whatever for?'

'Take you there, take you pack agaane,' explained the ancient. 'Chape, chape, too,' he added.

There followed a heated discussion: the nurse would give one shilling and not a penny more. At last the old fellow turned to his mate and said: 'A Dhia! Nach e an te ghrannd tha cruaidh!' (God! Isn't it the ugly one that is hard!)

This was too much for the nurse, who retorted in fluent Gaelic: 'Ma thi mi grannd a dhuine, tha mi onarach.' (I may be ugly, man, but I'm honest.)

Never, said Macdonald, had he seen an island gentleman so distressed and embarrassed. The shilling was accepted without more ado.

TRANSPORT

The difficulties and delays of transport in the Highlands – which can still occur despite the great improvements in the road system of recent years – have always been a source of humour, often of the stoical sort.

Until a ducal protest was uttered from Blair Castle, it is said that a stagecoach placard at the Duke's Arms Hotel in Dunkeld advertised the 'Duchess of Atholl' coach as follows:

> Every lawful morning at six o'clock, the Duchess of Atholl will leave the Duke's Arms and run non-stop to Perth.

*

One particularly fat Perthshire laird was accustomed to book two seats in the stagecoach, in order to fit himself in.

One day he asked a new servant to make the booking for him.

'Did you do it?' he asked when the man returned.

'Oh, aye,' said the man. 'But there was only the one seat left inside, so I took one on the top as well.'

*

A traveller in the Highlands was riding on the mail cart that ran between Achnasheen and Gairloch when the horses took fright at a rising bird and bolted. As he was bounced and rattled, he gasped: 'I'd give five pounds to get out of here.'

The driver, struggling to control the horses, was nevertheless able to shout back: 'You'll be out of it for nothing, at this rate!'

*

The Great North of Scotland Railway's line from Boat of Garten to Craigellachie was not notable for speed. On one occasion, a Kansas farmer on his way to Elgin to buy black cattle became highly discontented with the progress of the train. He complained vociferously to the guard each time he came by, until the official lost his temper and said that if he didn't like the train, he could always get out and walk.

'If I were in a hurry,' drawled the American, 'that's just what I would do.'

*

In the days when a branch railway line ran from The Mound to Dornoch, where it terminated, an anxious lady traveller changed from the main line to the branch train. Leaning out of the window, she asked a porter: 'Does this train stop at Dornoch?'

'If it doesna, mem, ye'll get an awful dunt,' he answered.

When the inhabitants of St Kilda were finally evacuated, in 1930, some of them settled for a time in Wester Ross. One elderly islander, intrigued by the comings and goings at the railway terminus of Kyle of Lochalsh, remarked: 'What's the use of that train going off to Dingwall every morning? It just comes back again every night.'

*

A brother and sister were returning from the Highlands to London, after their holiday. At Inverness Station, just before the *Royal Highlander* was due to set off on the long haul south, the brother decided to send a telegram.

'I won't be a moment,' he promised, dashing off.

His sister waited, becoming slightly alarmed as the porters began slamming the doors.

'All aboard, now, miss,' said one.

'Oh, but I'm waiting for my brother,' she said. 'Where's the telegraph office?'

'The telegraph office?' said the porter. 'It's too late to send him a telegram now – he'll never catch the train. It's away in two minutes.'

*

In the time of the Highland Railway, trains from the North stopped outside Perth at a ticket platform, for tickets to be checked before entering the station. Five men were sitting in one compartment. On the way, one had been fiddling absentmindedly with his ticket, and had finally dropped it on the floor. The man opposite, a bit of a joker, discreetly placed his foot on the ticket, then stealthily picked it up. When the train stopped at the ticket platform and the call: 'All tickets ready, please!' was heard outside, the absentminded one began to search feverishly for his ticket.

'I could swear I had it,' he muttered.

'Bad luck,' said the character opposite him. 'They'll make you pay the fare all over again.'

Then he offered a bright idea.

'Why don't you get under the seat here, and we'll hide you with our legs. The inspector will never see you.'

After some hesitation, the ticketless man squirmed and forced himself into the tight, dusty space beneath the seat. When the ticket inspector arrived at the compartment window, the joker held out two tickets.

'What's this?' said the inspector. 'Five tickets, but I only see four passengers.'

'The fifth one belongs to our friend down here,' said the joker. 'He prefers to travel under the seat.'

Before the bridge to Skye was built, a ferry ran between Kyle of Lochalsh and Kyleakin. One day a man on a bicycle came pedalling down the street of Kyle of Lochalsh in a great hurry, heading for the jetty. As he reached the waterfront, he saw the ferry about ten yards out. Seeing a plank laid at an angle on a herring box, he steered towards it, soared up into the air, and was just able to grab the side of the boat. A ferryman looked over with interest.

'Wow!' said the cyclist, holding the side of the boat with one hand and his bicycle with the other, 'that was a close thing.'

'Actually, we're on our way in,' said the crewman.

*

The climber Tom Patey recalled another ferry incident, when a careless crewman let a walker's rucksack drop into the limpid depths of a western sea-loch.

'Ach, James,' said the skipper of the ferry. 'You'll just have to be more careful next time.'

*

In the days before motors and regulations, the ferrymen often charged what the traffic would bear. Visitors were often asked to pay outrageously large sums by boatmen whose knowledge of English seemed to shrink in the face of complaints and queries. One traveller, being rowed across Loch Linnhe at Corran, was intrigued to hear the steersman of the boat constantly say to his two assistants: 'Fuirich, fuirich.' Paying the handsome amount requested, he asked: 'What does "*fuirich*" mean?'

The steersman looked a little nonplussed.

'Oh, it will be meaning, "Be careful now",' he said.

But as they were walking up the jetty, a fellow-passenger gave him a wry smile and murmured:

'It would be truer to say that "*fuirich*" means "Delay, slow down",' he said.

'But why should he say that?' asked the traveller.

'Oh, to make the journey a bit more worth your while,' said the other.

*

In the days when Macbraynes, the predecessor of Cal-Mac, had a virtual monopoly of West Highland transport, an anonymous author produced this quatrain:

> The Earth belongs unto the Lord,
> And all that it contains –
> All except the Western Isles,
> And that is all Macbraynes.

*

An islander on Eigg, when asked at what time the steamer would be arriving, said, after some thought: 'Weel, she'll be coming sometimes sooner, and whiles earlier, and sometimes before that again.'

The poet Ian Crichton Smith, in *Thoughts of Murdo,* put it more crisply: 'The Day of Judgement will be at hand when the Macbrayne steamer is on time.'

*

One of those steamers was the *Lochmor*, a familiar sight among the Small Isles, skippered for many years by the indomitable Captain Robertson. On one occasion, nosing in to Canna pier in a thick fog, the captain sent his mate down forward to the bows, to peer out into the mirk.

'Can you see anything, Mr Mate?' he called.

'No, captain, but I can hear ducks.'

'Can you see if they are walking or swimming? Because if they're walking, we're in trouble.'

*

The writer Alasdair Alpin MacGregor recalled his first voyage on the *Lochmor*, when the ship was forced to anchor in fog, in the Sound of Mull. The passengers on board, mostly tourists, became impatient and plagued the crew with questions.

'When do we arrive at Tabbamackie or something?' inquired one.

'A quarter to nine, *some days,*' replied a crewman.

'Is that a signal, or something?' asked another as the ship got under way again, and the same man hauled down the black ball signifying 'ship at anchor'.

'No, it's a Chreesamus decoraashun,' replied the much-tried seaman.

*

Another traveller recalled a particularly stormy trip out to Tiree on the *Fingal*. Even some of the crew were seasick. It seemed unlikely that any boat would put out from Scarinish to pick up passengers, but the lugsail ferry did come pitching out, and with great difficulty got a rope to the side of the heaving steamer. Sometimes she was up to the ship's rail, sometimes fifteen feet below.

'Is it safe to jump?' yelled the traveller to the captain.

'I wish to Tophet I had the chance,' he replied.

*

Another captain, whose English was tinged with Gaelic pronunciation, was hailed by a yachtsman as his vessel approached Kyle of Lochalsh.

'Skipper! I'm sinking.'

The skipper leaned out from the bridge deck, interested.

'And what is it you are sinking about?' he inquired.

A passenger for the Isle of Barra, arriving off the train at Oban one wild and windswept night, was somewhat disconcerted to see the modest size of the waiting steamer.

'Will that boat really take us out to Barra?' he asked a local worthy.

The Obanite drew himself up to his full height.

'That boat will get you to Barra tomorrow morning,' he declared. 'So long as nothing happens to Barra.'

*

Another intrepid traveller staying in Oban wanted to pay a visit to the Isle of Coll, and ascertained that the Macbrayne ship *Fingal* left for Coll and Tiree at 5 a.m. As it was before the days of alarm calls, he arranged that the 'boots' of the hotel would wake him up at 4.30.

'I'm a heavy sleeper,' he said 'Tell the boy to show me no mercy.'

He was duly wakened by a terrific battering at his door.

'Are you the gentleman that's going with the early boat?' a hoarse voice demanded.

'Yes, yes.'

'Well, *she's away,*' said the boots.

TRICKSTERS

In the Highlands, long ago and today, a smart man was and is respected, so long as his exploits can raise a laugh, and preferably leave someone else – who deserves it – deflated. Such men are of course also 'characters', but they are doers rather than sayers, and it is their actions that are remembered. One such was Somerled, the twelfth-century lord of Argyll, from whom the later Lords of the Isles traced their ancestry. Part Viking, part Gael, Somerled was a notable warrior. It is said that he fell in love with the daughter of Olaf, king of Man. At the time, Olaf was on an expedition into the Western Isles, to quell some rebels. Pretending to be a messenger, Somerled hailed the king's galley from the shore.

'I speak for Somerled, lord of Argyll,' he called. 'He will join your expedition and bring his men to help you. In return he asks for your daughter's hand in marriage.'

Olaf was not deceived for one moment.

'Let him join our expedition, by all means,' he said. 'As for the marriage, it is unthinkable.'

Somerled and his men joined up with Olaf. But Olaf's Hebridean foster-brother, Maurice MacNeil, was a close friend of Somerled, and together they made a plot. Maurice, a skilled boatwright, drilled holes secretly in the sides of the king's galley, and plugged them with wax. When the fleet put to sea, the wax dissolved, and the ship began to take in water. Soon the water was coming in faster than the ship could be baled out, and the crew were in distress. It was then that Somerled's ship appeared alongside.

'I will take you all on board,' he cried, 'once I have the king's permission to marry his daughter.'

With water mounting to the gunwales, Olaf was not slow to consent, and he and his men were taken on board Somerled's galley. His waterlogged vessel was towed to land, emptied, and patched. Knowing he was bested, the king honoured his promise.

*

Another tricky fellow who was long remembered in the West Highlands was the famous King Magnus III 'Barelegs' of Norway.

In the reign of King Edgar, son of Malcolm Canmore, the Scots agreed to the Norwegians' possession of the Western Isles. All the islands that a boat could be sailed round were granted to the Norse king. (His nickname, incidentally, has been put down to his adoption of Highland dress in preference to a Viking's tight breeches.) But, according to legend, Magnus also claimed the fertile peninsula of Kintyre. Sitting at the helm of a longship, its sails hoisted, he had himself dragged across the portage between East and West Loch Tarbert, thus constituting it an island. Although the event was believed to be historic fact in later centuries, it was untrue, one of the stories that accrete around a magnetic individual. But the Highlanders would have liked it to be true.

In old storytelling tradition, the trickiest character was one Mac-a-Rusgaich – a name which may mean 'son of the skinner', or 'son of the fleecer'. Either is quite appropriate. Mac-a-Rusgaich was up to all sorts of pranks. In one story, he hears of a farmer who is excessively harsh on his servants, and applies for work with this man. Each drives a hard bargain. The farmer stipulates one unusual condition – the first of the two to regret the bargain shall have a strip of skin torn off from the back of his head to his heel.

On his first morning at work, Mac-a-Rusgaich is told to go out to the moss and start digging peats. First of all, though, he asks for his breakfast, which is duly provided. Then he asks for his midday meal, so that he won't have to waste any time by eating it at midday. This too is provided, and then Mac-a-Rusgaich asks for his supper, so that he doesn't have to come all the way back for it. The supper too is made for him, and then he goes to see the farmer.

'What do your men do after they have had their supper?' he inquires.

'They take off their clothes and go to bed,' says the farmer.

So Mac-a-Rusgaich finds his bed, undresses, gets in and goes to sleep. By and by he is wakened by the angry farmer.

'Why aren't you out cutting peats?' demands the farmer.

'But you said, after supper your men go to their beds,' says Mac-a-Rusgaich.

After that, the farmer took care to give his new servant enough breakfast so that he could not possibly eat another meal after it. For another task, the farmer asks him if he can lay his hand to the plough?

'Indeed I can,' says Mac-a-Rusgaich.

'Then go and do so, in the dale down from the house,' says the farmer.

Obediently he goes and finds the plough there, and lays his hand to it as the farmer has asked. For a long time he stands there, holding the plough, until the angry farmer appears.

'Why are you not turning over the soil?' demands the farmer.

'I have laid my hand to the plough, as you requested,' says Mac-a-Rusgaich, 'and you can see for yourself that I am not letting her get away.'

'Adversities and calamities be upon you,' says the farmer.

'And upon you,' says Mac-a-Rusgaich, equably. 'Are you repenting of our bargain?'

'Oh, no, not at all,' says the farmer, hastily.

But the tricks go on until one day the farmer inevitably says: 'I wish I had never set eyes on you.'

Mac-a-Rusgaich offers him a choice – either he can pay three times the agreed wage, or else he must have the strip of skin taken off, as agreed. The furious farmer refuses to pay, and submits to the ordeal, but halfway through, the pain is too great, and he agrees to pay up. Mac-a-Rusgaich goes off jauntily to find new adventures.

*

Tricksters are not always human. The fox is a famous deceiver, in Gaelic tradition as in other European folklore. A story from Uist tells of a fox who had lost his tail.

One day the fox went out hunting with a wolf. Out on the moor they found a well-grown lamb, feeding some distance from its mother. Nearby there was a bog-hole. The fox told the wolf to come at the lamb from the other side and frighten it towards the hole. Meanwhile the fox hid himself in the heather until the lamb was close by and then rose up, scaring the lamb so that it fell into the muddy hole. When the fox came out of the heather, he was walking on three legs, as if he were lame.

'What is the matter with your leg?' said the wolf.

'Oh, I twisted it when I jumped,' said the fox.

When they went to the bog-hole, neither could reach the lamb at the bottom.

'You go down in the hole and pass the lamb up,' said the fox, 'and we will both have a feast.'

'Why don't you go down?' said the wolf.

'Oh, I am too lame.'

So the wolf went down, and passed up the lamb, and the fox immediately set to eating it.

'Help me out,' cried the wolf, feeling himself sinking, but the fox ignored him, and went on feeding.

'I'll have your head when I get out of this,' called the wolf, but the fox answered: 'Oh, leave my head, and grasp my tail.'

So saying, he caught up the lamb, presenting his tail-less rear to the hapless wolf, and went off, leaving the wolf to drown.

*

A MacGregor once played a helpful part in saving the life of a fellow clansman, who was being pursued by some vengeful Campbells, with a big black hound following his scent. The man had been chased down Glen Lochay to Loch Tay, then over the ridge into Glen Lyon (where he made the famous 'MacGregor's Leap' over the River Lyon and escaped). Encountering his fellow clansman on the way, he gasped: 'I am pursued by the black hound of the Campbells.'

'Have no fear,' said the other.

As the dog came bounding up, he killed it with one tremendous kick. When the Campbell men came up, he appeared innocently from the heather.

'Did you kill this dog?' they demanded.

'I swear that I never laid a hand on him,' said the MacGregor sincerely.

*

Highlanders share the general Scottish relish for deathbed jokes. One tells of a notorious robber of sheep and cattle, Donald MacGregor, who had survived against the odds to die a natural death. At the point of expiry, he was visited by the minister, who sternly invited him to repent, reminding him that all his crimes would rise up against him at the day of judgement.

'What?' gasped Donald. 'All the sheep and the cows, and the other things I helped myself to, they will be there in front of me?'

'Indeed they will.'

'Och, well, that will be all right, then,' said the sinner, relieved. 'Just let every gentleman take what is his own, and Donald will be an honest man again.'

*

William King, a prominent citizen of Kingussie, served with the Gordon Fencibles volunteer regiment in Aberdeen, early in the nineteenth century. On camp at one time, he was issued with cash to buy food for his men, but spent it on whisky. Then he realised that the mess officer was making a round of the various troops, to check on the catering. What to do? Then he remembered that a major in the regiment had a rather fine pair of chamois leather breeches. Quickly he sent a man round to abstract the breeches from the major's quarters, and stuffed them in the pot. When the mess officer came round, the pot was boiling nicely.

'Good pot today, King?'

'Yes sir, splendid pot,' replied King, raising the lid just a little. Back in Kingussie he enjoyed telling the tale: 'Agus cha robh ni 'sa 'phoit ach bhriogais o' mhaidsear.' (And nothing in the pot but the major's breeches).

WARFARE

John Roy Stuart, poet and Jacobite soldier, and composer of a memorable curse on the duke of Cumberland, celebrated his own escape after Culloden in a mock psalm:

> The Lord's my targe, I will be stout
> With dirk and trusty blade;
> Though Campbells swarm in flocks about,
> I will not be afraid.

*

When Prince Charles Edward Stewart was disguised as 'Betty Burke', the Irish maid of Flora Macdonald, he had some trouble in accommodating himself to feminine movements. His escort, Macdonald of Kingsburgh, had to ask him to moderate his long strides.

'Your enemies call you a Pretender,' he said, 'but if you be, you are the worst at your trade that I ever saw.'

*

Some of Prince Charles Edward's Highland followers were less than amused by the prayer offered up by the Rev. Mr MacVicar, minister at Duddingston, while the Highlanders were occupying Edinburgh in 1745:

'And for the man that is come among us to seek an earthly crown, we beseech Thee in mercy to take him to Thyself, and give him a crown of glory.'

In the height of the Somme campaign of 1915, the 51st Highland Division were transferred to a new and formerly relatively quiet position on the frontline. As they were preparing for the last stage of the move, one of the Jocks 'borrowed' a match from an army chaplain. As he lit his cigarette, he remarked: 'I've got something to tell you, sir. We've arrived, and ye're for hell noo.'

*

During the hot, dusty and hard-fought campaign in southern Italy in 1944, a young officer and his platoon of Highlanders were given orders to take an enemy position. About four hundred yards away, shimmering in the heat, the granite knoll looked unassailable. The lieutenant turned to his sergeant.

'Sergeant, how are we going to take that rock with fourteen men and a piper?'

The sergeant's brow furrowed momentarily, then he looked relieved.

'Well, sir, Corporal MacCallum is a damn fine piper.'

WEATHER

The oldest Highland weather joke is one perhaps shared with other hilly regions of the world, particularly localities which, like Dingwall, have a local mountain.

'When you can see Ben Wyvis clearly,' they say, 'it's a sign that rain is coming. When you can't see Ben Wyvis, then it *is* raining.'

*

'This is really awful weather,' said a visitor to an elderly resident of Tighnabruaich. 'What do you people do in all this rain?'

'We just don't interfere with it,' said the old fellow.

*

An engineer sent to Stornoway on a month's secondment found that his stay coincided with what seemed like perpetual rain. One day, setting out for work, he said to his landlady's little boy:

'Doesn't the weather ever change here?'

'I don't know,' said the child, 'I'm only six.'

*

For some Highlanders, the greeting 'It's a fine day' is so automatic that it escapes them even when the day is far from fine.

'It's a fine day, but coorse' is quite likely to be heard when the rain is falling and the wind is blowing.

*

The celebrated priest of Eriskay, Father Allan Macdonald, was walking in North Uist on a rainy day when he met a Free Kirk elder, and greeted him with:

'Not a very fine day.'

'It's the day God has given,' said the elder, unsmiling.

'It's not one of His best, then,' said Father Allan, passing on his way.

WHISKY

Whisky distilling probably began in the Lowlands, but now it is firmly identified with the Highlands. The Highland novelist Neil Gunn, who was also a whisky expert, noted an old saying of the country, 'the Highlander likes two things naked, and one of them is whisky'. But Gunn believed that a good malt is best dressed in a little water.

*

Hostess with bottle: 'How do you take your whisky?'
Highlander: 'Seriously.'

*

An aged and anonymous Highlander is quoted as saying, *à propos* of the national drink: 'Up to eight or nine is all right, but after that, it's apt to degenerate into drinking.'

Another of the same ilk remarked: 'Och, I will never think I have had a dram till I have had two.'

A development of this thought was in the saying:

One glass – neither the better nor the worse for it.
Two glasses – the better of them, not the worse of them.
Three glasses – the worse of them, not the better of them.

The glasses, of course, held a good deal more than the official fifth of a gill.

*

At many places in the Highlands, it is, or was, customary to offer a dram to a craftsman after the completion of a job.

After the plumber had installed her new washing machine, a farmer's wife offered him the usual, and he accepted. He watched carefully as she poured out a very modest quantity into the glass.

'It's ten years old, you know,' she said, sensing unspoken criticism.

'Aye, and small for its age,' said the plumber.

*

A grocer in Inverness, a good churchgoer, had a licence to distil whisky, 'for consumption on the premises only'.

Feeling that this cramped his trade, he was in the habit of selling jugs of whisky at the back door, and did very well out of it. The practice was well known, and one day the minister felt obliged to speak to him about it.

'You are breaking the law, after all,' he said.

He was given a long, serious look in reply.

'But I never approved of that law,' said the grocer.

And that was the end of the matter.

*

As a Christmas present one year, the laird gave Macphail, the gamekeeper, a deerstalker. Macphail was most appreciative, and wore the hat every day. When it was particularly cold and windy, he pulled the flaps down to keep his ears warm. Then one day the laird noticed he was not wearing the hat.

'Where's the hat?' he asked.

'I've given up wearing it, since the accident,' said Macphail.

'Accident? I didn't know you had had an accident.'

'Oh, yes. A man offered me a nip of whisky, and I had the earflaps down and never heard him.'

*

At Banchory on the River Dee, one of the local characters was 'Boaty', whose trade was to take anglers out on the river and guide them to the best pools. One of the perks of the job was to share in tots of the whisky, from the flasks which the visitors invariably carried, whenever a fish was taken.

One day, however, Boaty had a client who kept the whisky to himself, and this despite the fact that two good salmon lay in the bottom of the boat. After a while, Boaty began to pull for the shore, made fast, and began with calm deliberation to remove his gear.

'I say!' cried his client, 'what's going on? The day isn't half over.'

'Them that drinks by themselves, fishes by themselves,' said Boaty.

*

In the days when a landlord controlled the 'living' and could choose the parish minister, it was said of Lord Stormont, whose land covered several Perthshire parishes, that he only asked one question about a prospective minister: 'Is he good-natured in his drink?' If the answer was yes, the minister got the job.

*

'You know, whisky is a very bad thing,' said the district nurse to old Hector.

'Well, bad whisky is a very bad thing,' agreed Hector.

*

Two Highlanders were discussing a third, a recent arrival in their village.

'He's not a bad sort of a man,' said the first.

But the other disagreed.

'He's a mean man. Mean,' he said.

'How do you know that?'

'Well, I went to his house, just to say hullo, and he poured me out a glass of whisky.'

'Well?'

'And I said, 'Stop, now, that's fine.' And what do you think, he stopped!'

*

One laird of the old school, quoted by Dean Ramsay, contested that whisky was bad for the constitution, and even killed people.

'Na, na, I never knew onybody killed wi' drinking, but I hae kenned some that dee'd in the training.'

*

Between the Union of 1707 and the regulation and licensing of distilleries in the early nineteenth century, a period of more than a hundred years elapsed in which illicit distillation of whisky was rife in the Highlands, despite all the efforts of the government's excise men, or gaugers, to prevent it. No doubt many were caught, and no doubt some of the gaugers were smart men, but somehow all the best known tales celebrate the victories of the whisky makers.

Even the lairds supported the distillers and smugglers (indeed they were often the organisers of the activity). Archibald MacNab, after he had inherited the clan chieftaincy from the famous Francis, was asked one day to head a trial of some crofters who had been caught with a cartload of illicit whisky. One of his kinsmen, Dugald MacNab, explained to the new chief what should be done. On the day of trial, the MacNab demanded to taste the evidence. A barrel was brought in and opened. The chief took a sip and exclaimed: 'But this is water!' And so it was. In the dead of night, Dugald and his assistants had drained and refilled the barrels. The accused men were released, but the excise officers took care to bring no more cases before the new chief of MacNab, and to find a less partial judge.

Another celebrated Inverness whisky maker once took a consignment right past an excise 'ambush' while the revenue men solemnly removed their hats and placed them against their breasts. He was transporting the barrels in a hearse, under a black pall, with a coffin resting on top.

WORK

It has long been a jibe against the Highlanders that they are adverse to work. Even around 1500, a comic Highlandman could be made to say:

> So lang as I can get gear to steal,
> I never will wark.

This is of course an outsider's point of view. It is partly based on envy. People whose lives are governed by factory shifts, commuter trains and instant demands made via mobile phones are often rather jealous of people who seem to take their time about work. But there is a certain amount of evidence from inside to back it up. A Gaelic proverb says, 'It's a whole day's work, getting started.' Another says, 'When the Lord made time, he made plenty of it.'

A youth of sixteen was brought before the sheriff at Dingwall, on a charge of deserting his service from a farm at Dochcarty, nearby. Having been hired for six months, he had absconded after only three. When asked how he pled, he said, 'Guilty.' The sheriff thought he looked an honest type, and decided to enquire a little further into the matter.

'Tell me what happened,' he said. 'You look an upstanding sort of lad. What made you run away?'

His kindly tone brought tears to the boy's face, but he did not speak.

'Tell me in your own way,' prompted the sheriff.

'Well, sir, I went to the bit at Martinmas, an' I wasna lang there when the auld coo died. They sent me to town for a bag of salt, and I helped eat her.'

'Yes?'

'An' then, sir, the auld ewe died, an' they sent me to town again for salt, an' I helped eat her.'

'Yes?'

'An' then, sir, the auld sow died, an' they sent me to town for another bag o' salt, an' I helped eat her, too.'

'Well, that all seems reasonable enough.'

'An' then, sir, the fermer's wife's auld mither died. An' they sent me to town again for a bag o' salt. But I didna go back. That's how it happened, sir.'

*

A troupe of Glasgow actors was touring village halls in Argyll and having a very thin time. One day, one member of the cast rang his girlfriend.

'It's terrible,' he said. 'We had three sheep in the hall last night.'

'What did the audience do about it?' she asked.

'They were the audience.'

*

An old Highland tale records the experience of two men
from Kintail in Wester Ross, who set out to destroy a wolf
that was killing the crofters' sheep. One of the men had one
eye and was known as 'One-eyed Gilchrist'. They found the
wolf's den in a narrow cranny on the mountainside, and,
while One-eyed Gilchrist stood nearby, his companion went
inside. As Gilchrist watched, the wolf came running back to
enter its lair. He sprang down from where he was standing
and grasped it by the tail. The man inside called out:

'One-eyed Gilchrist,
Who closed the hole?'
Gilchrist replied:
'If the rump-tail should break,
Thy skull will know that.'

*

At the 'Best Ghillie' awards given out every year at a
certain estate on Deeside, Peter Grant won the 'Most
Tactful Ghillie' award for the third time in a row.

'How do you manage to do it?' asked an envious
colleague.

'Ach, man, it's easy,' he said. 'All you have to do is to
say to them: 'Man, you're a fine shot. The things you don't
aim at you hit just as easy as the things you do aim at'.'

*

Some of the basic facts of geology were established in the
Highlands, and geologists still come to the region. This
story is told of more than one, from the time of Sir Roderick
Murchison onwards. The geologist had spent an intensely
active day on Skye, collecting samples, and placing them in
his bag. At the end, he got a local lad to carry the bag back
to where he was staying, while he strode on ahead, enjoying
the evening walk over the moors. The bag was duly
delivered, but to his horror, when he examined the contents,

they were miscellaneous lumps of uninformative rock. When challenged, the boy confessed to having tipped out the bag and refilled it from a pile of stones near his journey's end.

'What is the difference?' he protested. 'Is the man not mad, to want a great bag of stones to be carried three miles, when there's just as many by his door?'

Sources for this book include:

T. Ratcliffe Barnet, *Highland Harvest*
Mary Beith, *Healing Threads*
J.F. Campbell, *Popular Tales of the Western Isles*
Robert Ford, *Thistledown*
Sir Archibald Geikie, *Scottish Reminiscences*
D.T. Holmes, *Literary Tours in the Highlands and Islands of Scotland*
Colin Macdonald, *Highland Journey* and *Highland Memories*
Alasdair Alpin MacGregor, *The Western Isles*
Emma Rose Mackenzie, *Tales of the Heather*
Angus MacVicar, *Salt in My Porridge*
Neil Munro, *Para Handy Tales*
Amy Murray, *Father Allan's Island*
Dean Ramsay, *Reminiscences of Scottish Life and Character*
David Ross, *From Scenes Like These: Scottish Anecdotes and Episodes*
Roland Wild, *MacNab, The Last Laird*
Transactions of the Gaelic Society of Inverness

and are gratefully acknowledged.